Advance Praise for ***Twenty Times I Almost Died***

"From Iraq to Israel, from the mountains to the jungle, John Spencer has lived through a vast array of experiences. Unfortunately for him, things have not always gone well. But fortunately for us, he has captured incredibly valuable lessons from his misfortunes and hardships. In *Twenty Times I Almost Died*, John shares these lessons and teaches us about discipline, perseverance, and ownership—and how to apply them to our own lives."

—Jocko Willink, (US Navy SEAL Officer, Ret.),
author of *Extreme Ownership*

"John Spencer has spent a lifetime learning what character looks like under pressure. In *Twenty Times I Almost Died*, he shows how moral courage is forged through hardship and why the distinction between good and evil still matters. This is a book not only about how one man was shaped, but about how others can be strengthened by his example."

—Douglas Murray, bestselling author of
On Democracies and Death Cults

"In *Twenty Times I Almost Died: Life Lessons from the Edge of Survival*, John Spencer tells compelling stories that illuminate the trials, tribulations, risks, and especially the rewards of service. Readers will gain an appreciation for the dangers of 'safetyism' and the disservice one does to oneself and others by avoiding the dangers and discomforts of life that produce growth, gratitude, and comradeship."

—Lt. Gen. H. R. McMaster, (US Army, Ret.), former
US National Security Advisor and author of *Dereliction of Duty*, *Battlegrounds*, and *At War with Ourselves*

"Respected author and urban combat expert, John Spencer, reveals the source of his wisdom—hard-earned personal experience—combined with insatiable curiosity. In a series of fascinating recollections, he entertains and instructs readers on everything from warfare to parenthood as no dry textbook ever could."

—Gen. Stanley McChrystal, (US Army, Ret.), former Commander of US and International Security Assistance Force (ISAF) Afghanistan and the Joint Special Operations Command (JSOC), and *New York Times* bestselling author of *My Share of the Task* and *Team of Teams*

"Ernest Hemingway couldn't have made up the real life of John Spencer. Facing Bullets, Bombs, and Bees (yes, bees, he was actually attacked by killer bees), Spencer writes about his adventures with humility, relatability, and humor. This book will leave you hungry for the next time he almost dies."

—Max Brooks, *New York Times* bestselling author of *World War Z*, *Devolution*, and the official *Minecraft* novels

20 TIMES I ALMOST DIED

LIFE LESSONS FROM THE EDGE OF SURVIVAL

JOHN SPENCER

BOMBARDIER BOOKS

Published by Bombardier Books
An Imprint of Post Hill Press
ISBN: 979-8-89565-556-6
ISBN (eBook): 979-8-89565-557-3

Twenty Times I Almost Died:
Life Lessons from the Edge of Survival

Cover Design by Jim Villaflores

BOMBARDIER
BOOKS

Post Hill
PRESS

Post Hill Press
New York • Nashville
posthillpress.com

Published in the United States of America
1 2 3 4 5 6 7 8 9 10

To Isaac, Izzy, and Maggie

Table of Contents

INTRODUCTION

MY LEFT EAR IS A natural conversation starter.

It is visibly damaged, about half missing. People get curious; they ask about it. It is a good story, and people's eyes tend to get wide. "Man, you could have been killed!"

"Oh, there's more where that came from." I smile, then casually mention this or that.

I was a soldier for twenty-five years, and now I am known in defense circles for my globe-trotting war research, teaching, writing, and public work. It is a life and career that has landed me in jeopardy a time or two. Or twenty.

Twenty times I almost died. Hard to believe, but here they are. Tales of war, of travels in unsafe places, training incidents, freak accidents that could have happened to anybody, and a few that were purely my own fault. The good, the bad, the weird. All autobiographical, but this is not an autobiography. These are stories about the moments that shaped me, about lessons that stayed with me long after the danger passed. The stories don't follow a timeline—they follow memory.

I brought a few values with me into the Army, as every young man or woman does when they raise their right hand and take an oath. But the truth is that I was reraised in the military. Every leader, mentor, and duty assignment molded me into who I am today. The Army did more than train me to fight. It gave me a deeper understanding of what it means to live by a code. I was shaped by people who taught me not just how to survive but how to lead, how to serve, and how to do what is right when no one is watching.

The Army instilled that ethos in me, and in many ways I was truly born the day I joined. That was the first step in becoming myself, and the values I hold dear were forged in my first years as an ordinary foot soldier. Each mentor, hardship, and test built another layer of character.

These stories are not all about that, but the lessons shine through in every one of them. If I have a mantra, it is simple: *Don't quit.*

That may sound easy to say, but it is true. It is almost unbelievable what you can accomplish by putting one foot in front of the other and knowing that another day will come. There is something primal about it, something built into our biology. No matter how deep the hole or how heavy the burden, if you take one more step, if you refuse to give up, you create the possibility of survival, of change, of victory. And that does not mean you never fall or fail. As you will see in these pages, sometimes you retreat, stumble, or take a step back. But quitting, truly quitting, is not an option.

I have worn many identities in my life: soldier, researcher, father. Each one has tested me in different ways and offered its own lessons. From combat I learned courage, resilience, and the importance of making choices under impossible pressure. From research I learned humility, curiosity, and the value of seeing things firsthand. From fatherhood I learned patience, compassion, and what *legacy* really means.

Every chapter in this book carries one of those lessons. Some are small, others are life-changing, but all of them are real.

I have three kids coming of age now, and while I do not expect them to follow in my warrior-scholar footsteps, if my life can serve as any example, it is this: You do not need to be fearless; you just cannot quit. The lessons of service, sacrifice, and perseverance are not just for soldiers. They belong to anyone willing to face life head-on, to carry the weight, and to keep moving forward.

I am also living proof that someone from nowhere can reach places they never imagined, simply by deciding to step out into the world and take action. To sample life beyond the familiar, to give yourself permission to take the big chance, and then to commit to it fully. Trying is important, but the principle of not quitting seals the deal.

This book is part of that same journey. Another hill I was not sure I could climb. But I am glad I did. Every close call left me with something worth keeping and something worth passing on. And yes, the ear story is in here. I will not spoil which chapter though, so happy hunting. Whatever you do, do not quit.

John Spencer

CHAPTER 1

EREZ

I AM NOT A SPY, but there are moments when I feel like I am living a Jason Bourne novel.

Take the brief email I got in December 2023. It came from one of my contacts in the Israeli Defense Forces, an invitation to join a small delegation near Erez, a main entry point into northern Gaza. I knew the place well. Erez is the primary humanitarian crossing point for Palestinian civilians commuting to Israel for daily work. I was staying roughly a ninety-minute drive north of there, at the Hotel Publica, one of the jewels in Tel Aviv's upscale northern district of Herzliya.

Two months before, on October 7, the terrorist network Hamas had launched the largest and most unspeakably brutal attack against Israelis, mostly civilians, in modern history, and Erez was one of their targets. The killers pillaged and burned much of the crossing point and killed a number of IDF soldiers.

As part of my military research, I was visiting the sites of October 7 as well as the various units both inside and outside of Gaza. I made it clear with a number of contacts that I was hoping in particular for a firsthand look at Hamas's extensive tunnel network. All

I had gotten in return, though, was a finger wag from my own government—from a "friend" who strongly advised I not go poking around a foreign flash point so controversial it had largely swept Russia's invasion of Ukraine out of the world's headlines.

My surprise IDF email invitation provided no details beyond an address and a meet time. Would I be embedded with a combat unit? What was our objective? What other factors might be in play? I had the option to decline—to kick back at the Publica's rooftop pool overlooking the Mediterranean, enjoy the fine dining, and stroll along the postcard-worthy Acadia Beach.

Of course, I took the plunge. It was my job, no doubt.

I have spent a fair amount of time working in Israel as a researcher and lecturer on national security issues, so I had no problem driving myself down the Route 20 highway to the designated rendezvous, which turned out to be a closed desert café, the last staging point before heading into Gaza. It was a beautiful day, but there was no mistaking the dull thud of not-far-off artillery.

It was easy to spot my fellow summoned foreigners. Most were seasoned authors and researchers like me. Some I knew by reputation, others from their book-jacket photos. The only other American was a woman who had that network-correspondent look: polished, handsome, a flowing mane of raven hair. Like the other nerds, I was surprised to learn she was in fact Debra Messing, from the hit comedy series *Will & Grace*. We chatted briefly; she was in Israel as a goodwill ambassador, touring sites of the October 7 attack and meeting survivors. With such a celebrity on board, I doubted our junket was headed for the front lines, although Ms. Messing and her bodyguard were sporting the same black helmets and flak vests as the rest of us.

Two government SUVs soon rolled up. And our host emerged from the lead vehicle.

I will call him Roei. He was a major in the IDF's Public Diplomacy section, what US troops would call a public affairs officer. I had known him for some time, so it was good to see him. He greeted us in excellent English, in what almost sounded like a Bostonian accent. Public affairs officers are not the gruff hard-asses who command troops in the field. Although I knew Roei's background as a dog handler in combat was nothing to scoff at. Most public affairs officers are more like corporate spokesmen—professional and knowledgeable, but affable, charming, and patient with civilian guests who may know little to nothing about what they are looking at.

Explaining we were to be shown damage just beyond the border, Roei ushered us to his vehicles, and we set off down a series of twisting desert scrub lanes. As the entry point facility came into sight, it was obvious we were sharing the approach with inbound IDF mech units headed for Gaza City to join the attack.

Pulling off the road near an admin building, we met the infantry squad assigned to accompany us. Roei addressed them in Hebrew, and they took us on foot past blown-open office facades, burned buildings, strewn rubble, and chilling evidence of small arms, grenade, and RPG fire. Heavy tanks and *Mad Max*–looking bulldozers rumbled right past us, while the artillery fire hammering the center of Gaza City was accompanied by the distinctive roar of Hellfire missiles fired from nearby helicopters. It was sobering, walking this close to the fighting, though what we were being shown was hardly the enemy infrastructure I had been hoping to study.

Once past the Israeli-side buildings, we were ushered through a giant gap in the border wall itself, and there was no doubt we were entering Gaza. Less than a hundred meters inside, we came upon a sandy hillside, and protruding from a dug-out area was what appeared to be an open end of a giant sewer pipe.

Roei halted us. That was no sewer. It was an entrance to an invasion tunnel. Hamas had spent years building a reportedly four-hundred-mile network under Gaza. What we were about to see was a main artery for funneling Hamas marauders to the very edge of the Israel–Gaza border.

"No civilians have ever been down here," Roei said. "You'll be the first, and you'll be the only."

I was anxious with anticipation in the knowledge I would gain, but calm. The rest of our party, not so much. People shifted uneasily, exchanged glances. It certainly was not any field trip Debra Messing had bargained for.

IDF forces had secured the immediate area, Roei added. Still, there were too many offshoot passages from the main tunnel to be guarded around the clock. Our infantry escort would be out in front of us at all times. Enemy contact was not expected, but possible. "Stay alert, stay alive," he concluded. That was a mantra I was very familiar with.

As the faces around me tightened, I considered our support squad. Mostly young men, a few women, making final checks of their weapons and gear, then their buddies', their faces taut as they muttered to each other in Hebrew. That is when I knew this was a tactical situation, not a dog-and-pony show.

When Roei gave the go, the squad members filed into the eight-foot black hole, their senses on high alert, fingers trigger ready, every slightest movement precise and calculated. The rest of us waited. I knew better than my colleagues what to expect. And even more about what to fear.

I should probably toot my own horn at this point—I am considered a leading expert on tunnel warfare. It is a subset within my broad area of study, urban warfare, but I can discourse on subterranean breastworks as far back as ancient times and have personally explored tunnels both in use and long abandoned in such far-flung locales as Iraq, Ukraine, Azerbaijan, and North Korea. So I can attest the minute we stepped through that hole, I knew it was like no tunnel I had ever seen.

It was too big. A normal Hamas tunnel is roughly one by three meters. This was easily twice or three times that, built extra wide to accommodate faster passage of larger groups of fighters and heavier equipment. Accordingly, it was more solidly constructed. Like most DIY projects, you can learn how to dig a tunnel by watching a few YouTube videos, but this could only have been designed, and the construction overseen, by a team of professional architects and digging engineers.

The initial walls were lined by curved steel plating, and pipes ran along the walls at ankle and shoulder height, carrying air, electrical cable, and likely commo wire. The stabbing sunlight pouring through the entryway revealed a steep downward slope before us. A ladder had been set in the ground, which descended to a length of metal grating, then finally a staircase. The steel walls continued as far down as we could make out. My snap estimate? Easily two years of full-time manual labor.

One by one, we started down the floor ladder, hand over hand.

The air was dank and foul, the passage cluttered with cast-off containers and refuse. After the ladder came a steel latticework, the width of a sidewalk, over which previous IDF patrols had laid a pathway of Kevlar blankets. Now we had to duck stray wires that hung from the walls and ceiling like tree moss. We were still backlit by the sun, but the troops farther down were now scanning every inch of the way forward by flashlight.

The air grew thick and stifling. It felt cooler as we went deeper, yet we were all pouring sweat. There was either no fresh air coming through the pipes or too many of us sucking up the limited oxygen.

There is also a basic human fear of dark, confined spaces. My fellow military scholars, veterans all, remained largely stoic, but the dread was apparent in Ms. Messing's wary bearing. Our Hollywood colleague had absorbed a litany of horrific testimony about the October 7 massacre, but venturing into the earth is fundamentally unnatural. Coal miners adapt to such conditions, but to most people, caves feel like entombment. Mythologically, the deeper you dig, the closer you get to hell. Which engineers might scoff at, but our brains are hardwired by instincts we never truly shake. Put simply, it was a nerve-wracking descent into the unknown, despite all of my previous experiences. No tourist walk in the park.

As Roei noted, we could be obliviously walking past camouflaged passageways, rooms, or ducts that previous Israeli patrols had not noted. And if there were not living, breathing terrorists about to pop out, who is to say they had not been there a few hours earlier setting IED tripwires? I had seen the worst of that in Iraq. Booby traps a child could assemble, yet lethal enough to take out an armored vehicle. And in this current war, too many IDF troops had learned the hard way about Hamas hiding explosives behind thin veneers of smooth concrete. We were all wearing protective gear, but bunched up close together in an enclosed, airless space? Even a small detonation would shred us like confetti. Everything in my experience signaled this was not a safe place. And being part of an ad hoc study group was not the norm for my research. It made me even more nervous, and I am not the nervous type.

I looked to Roei, hoping for some verbal or visual cue. How far was he taking us?

We kept on. It was cowboy-up time.

At last, the slope eased, and we emerged from the stairwell onto a relatively level floor. The walls here were the more traditional concrete reinforced with steel rebar. I estimated we were over a hundred feet down; Roei confirmed our actual depth as 150 feet. There was enough room down here to drive a vehicle through, and later-recovered home videos indeed showed the terrorists gleefully zipping about in a small pickup truck, which explained the extensive ventilation system: Without it, the carbon-monoxide exhaust would have been fatal.

Here we halted.

The guards were some twenty meters ahead, sweeping their lights about the blackness beyond. Again, I wondered how much farther Roei intended to go. Just walking around down here stirred up wafts of thick dust that contained who knows what toxins. No one in our group seemed eager to go much farther, and Ms. Messing definitely looked like she had had enough.

But my attention was locked on the soldier standing forward of us, his flashlight beam cutting into the void. Beyond him stretched more than two miles of unknown tunnel, running deep into the Hamas stronghold of Gaza City. Nothing about it was cleared or secure. Even if patrols had been here yesterday, or an hour ago, what waited beyond his light could change in an instant. The soldier was peering into uncertainty itself, into the possibility of an ambush, hidden explosives, or fighters slipping back into the darkness. The fact that we were even down there was, if I am honest, insane. Maybe I was the only one thinking it, but it struck me that while everyone else was glancing around uneasily, I could not take my eyes off that guard. His very presence at the front was the thin line between us and whatever Hamas might still have lurking inside the black.

I began visually collecting information. How the tunnel was constructed. What the builders had planned to do with it. This tunnel was estimated to extend two and a half miles back into Gaza City, and it was hard not to think about the people who built it. How long was it since Hamas fighters had been right where we were standing? The longer we lingered, the more uneasy I became. Nor was I much enamored of my group. Nice enough people, but if things went haywire down here, every nonprofessional in the mix would only put us at further risk.

Mercifully, Roei declared it was the end of the tour and explained why we were likely the last civilians to bear witness to it: Everything we had seen was marked for destruction. The thousands of hours, material, and money Hamas dumped into this pit would soon be utterly obliterated.

Exhaling in collective relief, we began to head back the way we had come. Photos were allowed as long as no soldiers were captured in them. The guards stayed in place, peering into the darkness as our herd filed back into the access passage. Retracing our steps up the forty-degree incline, nobody touched anything, and nothing blew up in our faces. Finally, gratefully, we emerged, huffing and puffing, on the sandy, hilly outskirts of Gaza City. The sky carried the haze of expired ordnance, plus a veritable sandstorm from the heavy vehicles still grinding past.

Two hours later, I was a world away, back in my room at the Publica Hotel, doing my best to shower off the dust, dirt, and who knew what else that clung to me. No, exploring the Erez Tunnel was not my closest brush with death. But after thirty years of putting myself at risk, I was starting to wonder just how long my luck would hold out.

LESSON: PRESENCE

If there is one lesson I carried out of this memory, it is the importance of presence. There is no replacement for it. Not in parenting, not in leadership, not in business, not in research, not in war. Titles and words matter but showing up matters more. A four-star general walking into a unit, Elon Musk on a factory floor, a parent sitting beside their child—presence communicates something that cannot be underestimated. The knowledge gained from presence, from simply being there, cannot be replaced.

In our connected global society, especially after surviving a pandemic, many have promoted the benefits of virtual substitutes. Zoom meetings, social networks, and video calls are valuable, but they are not the same. They cannot replicate the weight of human interaction, the unspoken signals, or the immersion of real experience. Presence communicates authenticity, respect, and commitment in a way nothing else can.

The same is true in business. When an employer shows up where an employee is doing the work, it not only signals that their time and effort are valued but it also provides knowledge that cannot be captured in a filtered report or a summary briefing. Standing beside someone on the factory floor or at their workstation reveals the process as it really happens, the challenges as they really unfold, and the issues that often get hidden or softened on their way up the chain. Presence shows people they matter, and it gives leaders a clearer picture of the truth.

I have learned this across every identity I have worn. As a soldier, presence meant walking the ground, standing with my soldiers in the mud and the danger, letting them know I was there too. As a researcher, presence meant entering the tunnels myself, whether Hezbollah's in Lebanon, North Korea's invasion tunnels, or Hamas's billion-dollar labyrinth under Gaza. Each was different, each carried its own danger, and each taught me something that no photo, map, or secondhand description ever could. Being there allowed me to connect dots across years and continents, to see how these networks were similar, how they were different, and what they revealed about the enemies who built them. That kind of understanding only comes from presence.

As a father, presence means something just as profound. It means sitting at the table, showing up for the game, being in the room when your child looks up for you. Just being there is often more powerful than any words of advice.

Presence carries weight because it is rare. It demands time, energy, and often risk. But it is also the one thing people remember most: not what you said, but that you were there. In my experience, in every walk of life, there truly is no replacement for presence.

CHAPTER 2

WELCOME TO THE JUNGLE

YOU MAY BE SURPRISED TO learn I was not *born* a warrior-scholar; my instincts in the Erez tunnel were honed by decades of on-the-ground (or underground) military experience. As my career has shifted into the realm of research and public engagement over the last decade, my interactions with actual foot soldiers—those young recruits who make up the backbone of all armed forces and perform all the necessary, often mundane, tasks of the lower echelons—was sporadic.

In Erez, our IDF support team are background figures. In a movie, they wouldn't have names or dialogue, but part of me remains highly attuned to what "the troops" are thinking and feeling. Once upon a time, I was a low man on the Army totem pole, and my first enemy contact occurred as far from Erez as you can imagine. Nor did it involve a desert or terrorists.

It was a jungle. In Central America. And those who sought to kill us were not human.

They took us by complete surprise. Wounded, we didn't even try to fight back. Just wheeled in panic, then hauled ass out of there as fast as we could. And it wasn't like we were untrained: They only sent us in after weeks of intensive classes regarding every possible danger.

But I was still a green kid. Seventeen years old, to be precise, newly assigned to my very first active-duty station as a private in the United States Army at what was then Fort Kobbe in the Panama Canal Zone.

Kobbe was home to my small airborne battalion and part of Howard Air Force Base. Our home was a peninsula surrounded by the shark-infested waters of Panama Bay, plus the untamed expanse of the Arraiján Forest to our west and north.

All of which provided a heavy dose of culture shock to a quiet, socially awkward teenager from Richmond, Indiana, a small city along the Ohio border. Meeting an Army recruiter at age sixteen, I was enthralled by his Ranger and Green Beret promo videos set to pounding hard rock, and I begged my hard-bitten single mom to sign the permission slip for their Delayed Entry Program. Within a year, I'd graduated high school, then Basic Training, Advanced Infantry Training, and Airborne School, my recruiter's recommended path into the Army's elite units.

That wasn't exactly true. There is no FastPass to joining the Best of the Best. I mean, I made it, eventually, but long before that proud day, I was riding in a Humvee, sweltering in the crushing humidity as we sped through the thronging, dystopian, sensory-overwhelming capital of Panama City. The most exotic place I'd been before was Disney World.

Once billeted, all Fort Kobbe newbies were prepped with a few weeks of jungle survival classes, and there was a *lot* for a young Hoosier to learn about:

Malaria. Jungle rot. Poison ivy.

Pit vipers. Poison dart frogs. Tarantulas. Leaf-cutter ants.

Vampire bats that flop down onto the jungle floor, then crawl up on their unwary, slumbering prey, and numb an area of your skin with toxic saliva so they can feed unnoticed.

Black-palm thorns. Razor-sharp, often the size of large nails, easily slice through clothing. Most thorns work their way out of punctured flesh, but black-palm thorns work their way *in*. Some are poisonous, and even those less immediately lethal can easily cause infection.

Wearing an Airborne patch suggests you spend most of your time up in the sky, basking in those twenty seconds of blissful parachute descent before the ground rushes up to slam your butt. In fact, we only jumped once or twice a month. Which was still a lot for an airborne unit. But far more of our Fort Kobbe time was spent humping bush as unforgiving as anything your granddad slogged through in Vietnam.

One item on the checklist to earn the mandatory Expert Infantry Badge was passing land nav—a.k.a. a land-navigation course, a.k.a. "hit the jungle with a compass and map and see if you can find a series of not-well-marked trees." I'd learned the basics in Basic; got a refresher at AIT. It's a day in the forest following your calculated azimuths to distant fixed points, plus keeping track of your steps to know how far you've gone. Take it slow and sure and it's actually kind of relaxing.

The Fort Kobbe course was *not* relaxing.

The jungle is primal, thick with growth you can't just sidestep, which throws off both your pace count and azimuth, and visibility is limited by the triple-canopy covering of the treetops. Shafts of daylight hit you in odd bursts of dazzling brilliancy that reduces all else to shadow.

At least they don't send you out alone. I was assigned a partner, whom I'd love to tell you about, but we'd never met before, rarely crossed paths after, and land nav doesn't lend itself to chitchat. So I'll just call him "Todd." Another white kid from the sticks, about my age, with no more jungle experience than I had.

They drove us out to the start point in two deuce-and-a-half trucks, and following a final safety briefing, we calculated our first direction of march and set off. Just getting from basecamp to our first marker was an ordeal. The temperature felt like a hundred, and we were wearing full BDUs, sleeves down, and helmets. No rucksacks but carrying an extra two-quart canteen each.

Given the number of times we lost sight of our fixed points, had to backtrack, then start over, it was like a miracle when we finally spotted Marker #1—a not-so-large, orange-and-white triangle nestled in the crook of a branch that looked like every other branch out there. We copied down the two-digit number written on the bottom and awarded ourselves a five-minute rest stop. Our uniforms were already plastered to our skin, and as we chugged water and mopped our faces, Todd fretted that finding four more markers would take us the rest of the day. Well, at least we knew where we were. If we dragged ass too long, we could find our way back out.

Our first distance had been roughly five hundred meters, but with all our detours and self-corrections, we probably walked twice that. Measuring the map distance to Marker #2, we determined it was over a kilometer away. Meaning, they let you start out easy. Now we had to be even more precise because in the dim light you could easily bypass your target by mere meters.

We calculated a new azimuth—the degree line to follow on the compass—and beat feet.

My first visual goalpost was, again, a gnarled tree branch, maybe forty meters out. I kept my eyes locked on the exact spot I'd sighted off of, while Todd handled our pace count (counting every step we took).

Progress was slow. Some clumps of undergrowth were simply impenetrable, and we'd no machetes to hack our way through. We skirted gullies, mud slicks, and uprooted trees. When the dense fern appeared before me, it looked like something I could sweep aside. Reaching in, I felt the main stem bend, and before I saw or heard anything coming at me, my face erupted in sudden and excruciating pain, like I'd been hit with a dozen flung metal-tipped darts.

Screeching incoherently, I stumbled back, arms flailing, but the wounds kept coming. Then the *sound* hit me: a buzz, a roaring cacophony of buzzing, and that's when it hit me:

Bees.

Incredibly pissed-off, swarming-to-attack bees. Desperately, I tried to swat them off my face, which only intensified what felt like searing flame. I lurched away, then somehow I was running, yelling to Todd—where was he? Then I saw him, abreast of me, and they were all over him like they were all over me, and we were both scrambling for all we were worth down what we hoped was the most easily navigable terrain.

I never ran faster. Legs pounding, head ducked, sleeves over my face, a tiny slit to see through. But the roar was still all around me, and little daggers were still plunging into my hands, the back of my neck, anywhere the dive-bombers saw exposed flesh.

How far did we sprint? Half a kilometer? It sure felt like it. Abruptly, we stopped, breath heaving, only to realize nothing had changed. They were *still* all over us.

Again, we took off. What else could we do? So we ran and ran and ran, what felt like a marathon but was probably another hundred meters, and at last that spine-tingling sound was gone, that creepy sensation of tiny wings fluttering against your aura.

I just about fell over. My face continued to burn and ache, and we didn't have anything to treat it. Todd was on his knees, like he was going to be sick, babbling profanity and disbelief.

In my agony, I remembered our classes and all the wildlife they'd warned us about.

Like the African killer bees.

And how the last thing you want to do is kill one. Because, on death, a killer bee releases a pheromone that acts as a distress call. Which summons the rest of the hive, whips them into a frenzy, and they aggressively kamikaze into any intruder foolish enough to arouse them.

What's a soldier supposed to do if swarmed? I couldn't remember my notes, just how surprised I was when they told us how many guys had *died* from bee attacks. Where I came from, getting stung was no fun, but it certainly wasn't fatal unless you were deeply allergic.

Todd and I lingered for some minutes. Breath still ragged, minds racing. Popped our canteens, splashed our faces like it was some miracle balm. It wasn't. When our first canteens shook empty, we drank from our seconds.

"What do we do?" Todd rasped.

I spit in the dirt. "Suck it up. Drive on."

"I dunno, dude."

I didn't know either. But one thing I *did* know: Ouchies or no ouchies, if we staggered back to the rally point having found only *one* friggin' marker, the hulking, ornery, Latino bandito of a master sergeant who ran the course was going to smoke us from here to Kingdom Come.

What I most dreaded was being noticed. Attracting attention. From the day I enlisted, I'd always tried to be the gray man.

I dabbed my face. Was it swelling? "We should find another point."

Todd didn't look too sure about that.

And then it slowly dawned on us. We didn't actually know where we were. How far had we gone during those two breakneck dashes? Should we find our way back to the hive, our last moment on the proper azimuth? It seemed impossible. Not to mention stupid.

Nor could we easily find our way back to that first marker. Within the borders of the course, our map was essentially blank; no terrain features to reconnoiter from. Slowly, we both pivoted, trying to make sense of the gloom and tangled foliage.

Every direction looked identical.

So now we weren't just frazzled, exhausted, sweat-drenched, and hurting. We were *lost.*

We stood helplessly for another minute. Wracking our jungle-virgin brains for any ideas.

Todd finally shook his head. "Take the panic azimuth, I guess."

Yeah, we had a "panic azimuth," the designated compass degree to lead us back to the course boundary road from any point within. People got lost out here all the time, the training sergeants warned us, and the Army wasn't about to call in a Search & Rescue for every Snuffy.

I sure didn't see any other way. We could tramp around out here until the sun went down and never get *near* another marker.

The panic azimuth was listed on the map. I took a site on it, and off we trudged.

The slog was miserable. After twenty minutes, we stopped to hydrate, but now my second canteen was empty too. Why had I wasted it splashing my face? I looked to Todd. He was down to a few drops as well.

We kept on. Every footfall a fresh jolt of pain. All in all, it was more miserable than any previous bad day I could recall.

Finally, the foliage and the shadows parted, and we stepped onto what had to be our road.

We were so disoriented that it took a minute to figure out which way led back to base camp, but logic finally prevailed. Setting off anew, we prayed for any passing vehicle to flag.

There were none.

Finally, *way* off down the road, we saw a semicircle of vehicles around a GP admin tent where we'd arrived. By now, I could barely see straight. I was dizzy, light-headed, fatigued. My stomach ached. It didn't make sense. I wasn't allergic to bee stings, so why did I feel so sick? Maybe it was heat exhaustion, exacerbated by dehydration. They drummed that stuff into you on a daily basis in the tropics. Now I knew why, and I was scared. Any soldier deemed a severe heat casualty at Fort Kobbe was a marked man. I mean, they literally tagged you with colored warning tape, which was the last thing *this* gray man wanted or needed.

When we finally reached the area, I knew I had to sit down. There was a lean-to off to the side of the tent for a portable generator, and I took a seat behind it, the putt-putt of the motor a kind of ordering pulse for my jumbled thoughts. Todd kept walking—I don't know where. To lick his wounds somewhere in private. I saw him later, on the Deuce, but neither of us felt like hashing it over.

One thing a private cannot get away with in the Army is to sit and do nothing, yet any number of course instructors saw me sitting there cross-legged over the next hour, and not a single one of them hassled me. No one seemed to know or care that we had abandoned the course or run into trouble. For whatever reason, I just sat, and after some time, my head cleared a little. I refilled my canteens at the lister bag and felt slightly better, at least enough to get back on the truck when the day was done.

As we jostled back and forth on the hard bench seats, I thought back to those way-cool Special Forces videos I saw in Indiana. Rugged, square-jawed men rappelling out of helicopters, scaling cliffs, bridging chasms, and leaping from rubber boats into the foamy surf. I bet guys like that never got their butts kicked by a bunch of bees during land nav.

Maybe the jungle was trying to tell me something. That maybe I was not ready to take on the whole world quite yet. Maybe I needed to dig deeper if I wanted to be the Best of the Best.

Yeah, the bees won that round. No question about it.

And while none of the instructors said a word about my performance that day, flying under the radar did not save me from my team leader. He had me cranking out push-ups, jumping jacks, and sprints, all while laughing at the angry red welts swelling across my face. That was the Army for you. No mercy, no excuses, and sometimes a reminder that no matter what stung you out there, you were still expected to get up and keep going.

Thing is, though, I was no quitter. If our superiors wanted us back out there the next day, I would be there. With a big smile. Sucking up the pain, ready for whatever might come flying at me.

LESSON: PERSEVERANCE

Perseverance is persistence in doing something despite difficulty or delay in achieving success. But not quitting is not about foolishly putting your head down and charging blindly through every obstacle. Perseverance is not a refusal to ever change direction. It is about making wise choices in the face of risk.

I learned throughout my career that there are many forms of risk. There is always danger, whether in combat, in life, in business, or even in parenting. Risk of injury, risk of failure, risk of mission loss. The military has a concept called prudent risk, which means you assess the situation, weigh the potential outcomes, and decide what is worth it. That same calculation carries over to every role in life. A good soldier, a good leader, a good parent, even a good researcher, is always assessing risk.

That day in the jungle, perseverance meant knowing when to move forward and when to step back. We made a calculation that continuing down the path meant a possible deadly reaction from the swarm of killer bees. We were not allergic, but even without allergies a swarm can kill. So we did not push ahead. We retreated, recalculated, and then kept going in a different direction. That was not quitting. That was perseverance.

This lesson carried over into so many parts of my life. In combat, retreat can be the wisest move to preserve your force and fight another day. In business, abandoning a failing path is often the only way to find a better one. In parenting, knowing which battles not to fight can be the difference between chaos and calm. Perseverance means continuing on the journey, even if that means adjusting your route or taking a step back.

Risk is a part of life. The key is not to confuse perseverance with recklessness. Not quitting does not mean you never stop, never retreat, never abandon a plan. It means you keep going, with wisdom. That was one of the first lessons I learned in that jungle, and one that has guided me ever since.

CHAPTER 3
CANAL

THE BEES STRUCK US WITH overwhelming force. They routed us from our position, degraded our combat effectiveness, and left us demoralized. I would not experience such a relentless attack for another decade. Thankfully, when it came to pass, I was one of the aggressors that time.

This is the story of my first firefight against enemy troops in a theater of war.

The place: northern Iraq. The time: the opening days of Operation Iraqi Freedom.

I'd come a long way from being that green kid in Panama. Steadily advanced through the enlisted ranks, to sergeant first class, and earned my coveted Ranger tab along the way. Best of the Best, as I'd always aspired to be. Only the higher I climbed, the more my duties involved admin and planning rather than leading men. I wanted to stay in the field, not fly a desk somewhere, so I applied for Officer Candidate School.

A long time ago, military officers came from the ruling classes. They delighted in fancy uniforms, fine dining, pomp and circumstance. They were not noted for any great concern with the well-being of their troops, who were generally recruited from the peasantry or the dregs of society, and those in charge may or not have been able to command their way out of a paper bag.

Thankfully, the United States has increasingly supported the tradition of a professionally trained officer corps, and birthright and wealth are no longer the cornerstones of leadership. Even so, a cultural divide still exists between the upper and lower ranks. Most male officers today are trained in college through ROTC or at one of the elite service academies. They have never served as regular soldiers, let alone the eight years I had in.

My background generally earned the goodwill of my men, but there's always an initial wariness when a new officer takes command. As a newly minted second lieutenant, I was now leading a platoon, roughly forty men who didn't know me from Adam. And all of us were parachuting into a hostile foreign land halfway around the world to defeat their armed forces.

Thankfully, our night drop into Iraq encountered no enemy resistance. It was tough enough carrying a hundred pounds per man as we hopped out of a monster C-17 Globemaster cargo plane into the inky, rushing roar of the unknown. We thought the Middle East was going to be all *Lawrence of Arabia*, but there were no blowing sand dunes or camels waiting for us below. This was northern Iraq, closer to the Turkish border than to Baghdad, the climate a temperate grassland. Unbeknownst to us, it had also been raining for the past week, which turned our landing-zone plain into a mud flat. By that point in my career, I'd parachuted over fifty times and graduated from one of the Army's toughest schools as a qualified jumpmaster. But for a lot of newbies, it was only their sixth time out the door, following the required five at jump school.

So there we were. A thousand men, scattered over farm fields in the dead of night, staggering under excessively loaded rucksacks across sodden ground in search of our designated assembly areas. Had we to contend with sweeping searchlights and raking machine-gun fire, it would have been catastrophic. As it was, some men were simply overwhelmed. Disoriented, physically spent, they sprawled where they landed, waiting until daylight allowed their units to provide aid.

From that inauspicious beginning, we managed to constitute ourselves and establish a secure area of operations as we awaited the vehicles, equipment, and heavy weapons being delivered to the airfield we'd been tasked to secure. Aside from some friendly Kurdish fighters, we had no contact with Iraqi forces or civilians, allowing us precious time to acclimate, rest, and prepare for future action. Only one warning from Intelligence came through: a column of enemy tanks headed our way.

Tanks?

American infantry hadn't gone toe-to-toe against heavy armor since Desert Storm. We scrambled into readiness, establishing interlocking defensive positions with anti-tank guided munitions. We felt confident we would repel whatever came rumbling our way, then exhaled in relief when the warning turned out to be a false alarm. Real or not, it was our first jolt of anticipatory adrenaline: that this wasn't all some elaborate field exercise. It was a real war, and we were *way* behind enemy lines.

Two days later, amidst a torrential downpour, my fellow platoon leaders and I were summoned by the company commander, and the larger strategy and purpose we'd been briefed on became a reality. The Coalition's main attack would be a race to Baghdad from the south. Meanwhile, Saddam had divisions in the north, near the cities of Mosul and Irbil, just south of us. Our job was to stir up enough trouble to keep those northern Iraqi forces from speeding south to reinforce the dictator's besieged capital. Accordingly, our first mission was to attack an enemy division headquarters.

In war movies, briefing scenes are usually low-key. An older character actor describes the plan as his subordinate leaders puff cigarettes, take notes, and offer sardonic quips. Our meeting was anything but blasé; the collective unease was palpable. Again, we were American soldiers preparing to unleash deadly force against an opposing army. Since Vietnam, that had only really happened in Grenada and Panama back when we were kids, then Desert Storm a dozen years before. Careers devoted to preparation and readiness were now to be put to the test.

In a nutshell, my mission was to establish an artillery battery firing point that would engage the enemy, with a few platoons deployed some distance ahead in order to deter any Iraqi counterattack. These forward units were to form a line within sight of the enemy trenches and bunkers, set out wire and warning signs for any civilians, and support the incoming barrage with direct fire.

It felt like more needed to be said, but with no actual combat veterans among us, who were we to judge the level of detail? What was more interesting was realizing I was the Old Man among the platoon leaders. I'd never fought in a battle, but with all my years directing men and materiel in training scenarios, the next planning steps came more instinctively to me than others. I had four hours to determine our route, order of march, and final positions, then make sure my men were squared away. I placed my own platoon at the head of the column, with my personal Humvee in the lead. It wasn't for glory, but to assure I'd have eyes on whatever lay ahead and not have to make decisions based on a game of telephone. It was the right call, and it almost got me and my crew killed before the battle even started. But we'll get to that.

We were to travel by road, with no lights, just by night vision goggles, which at that time illuminated the world in a blurry green hue with terrible depth perception. We wouldn't be blind in my lead vehicle, but I sure hoped my driver, Ralston, had eaten his carrots. Behind him sat Meyer, on fire support. Cathcart, our radio man, sat behind me, and standing between all four of us was Brooks, who manned the heavy .50 caliber machine gun up top. All four were young enlisted men, sons of the South, and after two weeks riding with them, I felt we had a decent working rhythm. That too would pay off down the road.

But let's get back to the mission.

Our road south would cross a major bridge, then continue another kilometer to a crossroads, where I would deploy my men and vehicles along the bisecting road. One detail bothered the hell out of me, though: that business about setting up wire and warning signs. Higher headquarters really thought that was necessary? Whom were we supposed to be warning? Civilian lookie-loos sashaying up in the dead of night? I debated asking for clarification, then hoped that aspect would be scratched, but no, a supply truck turned up to unload rolls of concertina wire and large, prepared signs. I can't read Arabic, so I assume they said, *"Stop! You are entering the Kill Zone! Do not pass Go! Do not collect $200!"*

When were we supposed to put up these decorations? Once my men were in place along the road, we had to begin our attack, not wait around for some Iraqi patrol to raise the alarm. A more cynical officer might've "forgotten" the wire and signs, but I simply decided I'd handle that part myself. A good leader does not build unit cohesion by passing the stupid on down the chain.

Near midnight, our operation was ready to roll. My eight heavily armed and mostly open Humvees led the way, followed by supporting infantry riding in deuce-and-a-half trucks, then a convoy of fifty vehicles that would halt two kilometers from the enemy to set up and support the artillery.

Our progress was steady, if slow. In a Humvee, you can't feel the difference between pavement and ground, so we really had to watch and make sure we were on the road. At least the rains had let up, so I wasn't worried about getting mired.

The night was clear, and time passed in thoughtful contemplation of the upcoming mission. The soldiers always had questions. The four in my vehicle had special access to "the LT." Questions ranged from what we were doing to what we wanted to eat when we got home.

I cut the chatter when we got within a few kilometers of the enemy. We needed silence to focus on the mission, though it noticeably increased the already high tension. We hit a dip in the road, which was more like a gully no one had thought to mention, then we were climbing out of it again. I figured we'd reached the bridge until Brooks started yelling in panic.

"*Stop! Stop! Stooooop!*"

Ralston, no fool, did as advised, and the vehicles close behind us followed suit. Squinting out the windshield into the darkness, we saw the ground ahead appeared to be *in motion*. And then we realized it wasn't ground at all.

It was water.

We'd reached the bridge all right but had somehow gotten off the road and were now beside it, not on it. I hopped out to inspect our predicament. The dip had taken us to a canal that looked deep and wide, and our front wheels were clinging to the last few inches before a straight drop down. Had Brooks been dozing, we would've gone over, and even if the impact hadn't broken all our backs, it's hard to believe any of us would have survived the plunge. Unfortunately, there was no time to celebrate not being dead: As the leader of the pack, my whole parade had closely followed us to near disaster. Now we were bunched up tight with no way forward, and still under blackout conditions. We needed to un-muck ourselves, pronto.

One of my best sergeants became the man of the moment. Hopped out, took the reins of traffic control, and miraculously herded every vehicle back up to the road and across the bridge.

Later, I'd have all kinds of time to play woulda-shoulda-coulda regarding our near-fatal mishap, but we still had a battle to get to. Another kilometer down the road, we hit our assigned intersection, and I radioed my vehicles to their positions. The trucks spread in opposite directions in a maneuver that looked like we'd rehearsed it a thousand times. We *had* practiced, but I had no idea how it would work on the ground. Then the trucks of infantry arrived, and the men dispersed in both directions to fill the gaps between my Humvees. Two hundred meters before us was the enemy position, a mix of bunkers, trenches, and outbuildings.

Two of our grenade launchers first broke the stillness, then every weapon we had opened fire, soon joined by the incoming whine of the artillery shells over our heads, and then we heard the earth-shuddering detonations. I'd seen mass-fire demonstrations, so-called million-dollar minutes, but the for-real version was spellbinding. With Sergeant Meyer and the spotters directing our fire with pinpoint accuracy, we hit the enemy with overwhelming force. It seemed impossible anything downrange would live to fight another day.

Amidst the wonder, I suddenly remembered I hadn't set up any wire or signs. Grabbing my radio man, Cathcart, we wrestled the supplies off the front of the vehicle where I'd tied them down. Trotting down the road about twenty meters, we threw the signs and spools of wire on the ground. I had no intention of setting anything up, but at least I could check the box on this particular task. The Iraqis, following their initial shock, had begun firing back at us with machine guns, only it was clear from the glow of their outgoing tracer rounds that they couldn't tell where the mayhem was coming from. It was about then I heard my first *crack.* I'd been told closely passing bullets make that distinctive sound—as opposed to a *zip* when they're farther away—and my reaction was surprisingly calm. Less "Oh, God," and more like, "Well, *that* just happened." Was it the same for the rest of my guys—all those kids fresh out of jump school?

Things got more interesting when Iraqi mortar shells started to fall and burst in our vicinity, which made the comedy of putting up warning signs even more absurd. Cathcart and I jumped back in the vehicle, and I continued my actual job of commanding the platoon. Some of my squad leaders were requesting permission to advance, but this was not a raid. Our job was to hold this line, then pull back. If anything, I was worried we were firing too much. You never want to go black on ammo, i.e., shoot all you've got and leave yourself defenseless.

Suddenly, a more urgent call came through. An enemy vehicle had been spotted speeding down the road, heading toward our line's left flank. Which was where Cathcart and I happened to be. We looked about, couldn't see or hear anything, and calculated our chances of repelling whatever it was with Brooks's .50 cal. I was still straining my eyes when my goggles suddenly flared into blinding white light. Dumbfounded, we saw a burning army truck about four hundred meters away. One of our mortar teams had fired on it by line of sight, a.k.a. "direct lay." As a former mortar man, I could only marvel. It's incredibly difficult to accurately fire a mortar that way; a direct hit, on a moving target, was astounding. Thankfully, that was as close as I came to meeting the enemy face-to-face that night. For a first battle, it was close enough.

When our spotters determined the enemy emplacements had been completely destroyed, and the Iraqi survivors were fleeing on foot, I received the order to collapse our position, and we began to pull back in the reverse order we'd arrived. Amazingly, I took zero casualties that night. Everyone who came out was going back in one piece. My eight vehicles became the rearguard as the artillery battery was packed up and moved out, and again, thankfully, no one roared up out of the dark to challenge us.

That was my combat debut as a platoon leader. I overwhelmingly respected the conduct and actions of my men and felt they respected mine in return. It was a feeling expressed more in looks than words, but a solid floor of institutional trust had been established.

And all those thoughtfully prepared warning signs and that nicely coiled razor wire?

As far as I know, they're still out there.

LESSON: COMMON SENSE

The US military is full of maxims, principles, and rules, from Sun Tzu's sayings to the principles of war. They are handed down as lists, memorized by generations of soldiers, often without anyone knowing exactly where they first came from. But they endure because they work. They are lessons that, despite context, prove useful more often than not.

One of those lists I learned as a young soldier was the five principles of patrolling: planning, reconnaissance, security, control, and common sense. At first glance, "common sense" might seem too obvious to even include. But over the years I came to understand why it earned its place right alongside planning and security. Common sense saves lives.

This story was proof of that. Common sense was my gunner recognizing the danger of the canal and halting us before we drove into it. Common sense was the driver reacting immediately, even if it meant breaking rank and ignoring the hierarchy, because survival demanded it. In a perfect organization, common sense is instinctively trusted, but in reality, many systems fail to value it. Orders are followed, checklists enforced, and sometimes that rigidity puts people at risk.

There was also the common sense of questioning orders that made no sense in the moment, like being told to throw out signs during an operation when it was clear it put us in greater danger. Following orders is a duty, but that duty does not mean abandoning judgment. Time and again I have seen that the difference between disaster and survival comes down to someone deciding to speak up or to act differently because what was ordered defied basic common sense.

This lesson has carried through my life in uniform, in research, in leadership, and even in parenting. People are human. Rules and structures are important, but they are not infallible. Sometimes the best thing you can do is stop, think, and say, "That doesn't make sense, so we are going to do it another way." I cannot count how many times that simple act of trusting common sense saved my life or resolved a situation before it spiraled out of control.

CHAPTER 4

THE YELLOW CORD

YOU KNOW THE STORY.

Saddam surrendered six days after we invaded Iraq in 2003. All his forces laid down their arms. Many of them literally took their clothes off in their positions and walked away, leaving both their clothes and weapons behind. Coalition forces left the major population centers while Iraq adopted a bustling new democracy. It was a great feeling for us up north, having entire cities cheering and coming out to touch us or our vehicles as we finished our drive to the city of Kirkuk. They came out with smiles and laughter when we opened a new medical clinic or donated backpacks and soccer balls to a school.

By the Fourth of July, we were all back home in the States, firing up the family barbeques and telling war stories.

OK, that is not what happened.

A lot of people think the Iraqi insurgency only erupted a year later, but in fact we were battling an array of irregular forces even before President Bush stood before his taken-out-of-context or spoke-too-soon "Mission Accomplished" banner on May 1, 2003.

It is true that Saddam, his sons, and other top leaders went into hiding and that regional leaders all across the country surrendered their offices. Most of the regime's men in uniform, be they military, police, or other enforcement agents, publicly shed their uniforms, but few actually laid down their arms. Instead, they carried them back to whatever city or hamlet they called home, and thus became the backbone of every militia, terrorist cell, and street gang to come.

Without the Iraqi Army to fight, Coalition duties shifted to assignments intended to stabilize a suddenly ungoverned country of twenty-four million people. We tried to keep order, and we supported humanitarian efforts, like escorting water and cooking-gas trucks and supervising distribution. We collected intelligence. Who were the bad guys in our sector, and what were they up to? We also conducted manhunts, pursuing those fifty-two Most Wanted senior Baath Party officials, the men with their names and images famously printed on decks of playing cards.

Inside our encampments—the larger ones called Forward Operating Bases (FOBs), the smaller ones Combat Outposts (COPs)—we felt relatively secure. Our new enemies would fire rockets and mortars our way but rarely dared to confront us directly. Instead, they began asserting their presence on the long stretches of empty road between our bases. Within a month of our boots hitting the mud, the insurgents were deploying improvised explosive devices, soon to be famous worldwide as IEDs. It was too risky for terrorists to engage American infantry in a gunfight, but they could take out two or three of us with homemade bombs while we were driving around.

Our Humvees looked rugged, even fearsome when augmented with heavier weapons, but they were only designed to ferry men and equipment around the battle area, like the jeeps back in World

War II. Humvees were not armored and quickly became the bad guys' favorite target.

The bombs in 2003 were not the sophisticated, high-tech devices we saw in the years to come. They were crudely designed and assembled, which did not make them any less lethal. It was worse for troops occupying the cities, where literally any piece of refuse in the street might be concealing a booby trap, but out in the hinterlands, we quickly learned to be wary of dirt piles, animal carcasses, or broken-down vehicles conveniently close to the road. It was not that we could not travel without being attacked—just that things could, and did, happen. "Stay alert, stay alive" became our new daily affirmation.

As a platoon leader, I had to get my men and vehicles to certain places at certain times. In an optimal world, any road we used would have been inspected by an Army bomb squad—EOD, explosive ordnance disposal—on a daily basis, but there were hardly enough of them. Instead, officers at my level sent out squads of regular soldiers to scan the roads for anything suspicious, even though, frequently, we could not spare the manpower either.

The afternoon I will never forget began with a briefing at a Forward Operating Base about twenty miles away. I was not worried about the drive there. The wagon train of my eight Humvees was a daunting sight, and the largely uninhabited crop fields, grazing land, and crisscrossing canals we passed did not offer much cover for enemy snipers.

Some of the guys you met in chapter 3 were still with me. Specialist Cathcart was still my radio operator, and Private First Class Brooks continued to man the .50 cal., but I had already gone through a few drivers. Maybe I could have been more polite when screaming directions in their ears. "*Take a left! Up there! Your other left, Magellan! Slow up! Now punch it! Get us out of here! Go! Go! Go!*"

Anyway, that day, Brooks saw the stranded vehicle before we did. Nothing unusual there. Iraq was full of paint-flaking junk wagons any DMV in the States would have sidelined. The one we were approaching was a late-sixties-model Citroen with the hood propped up. The driver had pulled off the road beside a fallow field and was presumably making repairs. A shawled woman and a little girl stood by, squinting as we slowed and passed them. The husband was indeed huddled over the engine, and nothing appeared amiss.

For a split second, a voice in my head told me to stop. Just a split second of something. We had developed a practice of stopping to check out these stranded cars for anything nefarious. But today we were on a clock, and without even uttering a word my decision was taken. We were past the spot. That was decision number one, and even at the time I knew it was not logic that tugged at me. It was intuition. Fifteen minutes later, we arrived at the FOB as scheduled, and the full company briefing went down without a hitch.

Two hours later, we departed, returning to our battalion headquarters by the same route.

The day was clear, though the wind had picked up, and there looked to be a storm brewing out along the northern horizon.

Again, it was PFC Brooks who ruined the party: "*IED! Stop!*"

The column slowed, my every soldier now scanning his assigned fire sector for any hint of an ambush. But the barren flats all around us suggested nothing.

As our wheels came to a halt, Cathcart wondered, "Isn't this where we saw that car, sir?"

I looked around. It was hard to tell. If this was the place, there was nothing around now.

I swept both sides of the road with binoculars, but Brooks had better vantage. "Can you see anything, PFC?"

"Looks like a wire, sir. Coming out of the dirt, on the right there. Going across the field."

I found what he meant. It was a wire. With yellow insulation. Bright yellow. That alone was peculiar. I had seen my share of IEDs. The wires were usually black or subdued colors.

Following the yellow line, I saw it indeed led to a dirt mound right beside the road, which was undoubtedly concealing a half-buried artillery shell. And, sure enough, there were fresh tire tracks. Meaning Mr. Goodwrench was Mr. Bad Guy, with that lady and her kid stuck out there as decoys. Once again, eagle-eyed Brooks had saved our butts by spotting something we would have never seen, and how lucky were we that Joe Terrorist had not bothered to camouflage his trap.

We sat a minute as I debated our options. One of those moments I felt four pairs of eyes on me, waiting to see how I handled it.

"I can guess what's beside the road. What I can't figure out is where that wire is going. There's nothing out there." I was musing aloud, not inviting opinion, but I heard a murmur of agreement. I finally decided. "Let's drive around to the far side. See if we can see anything." We turned onto the field, eased along what I hoped was a safe path, staying parallel with the cord. When I felt we had driven far enough, I ordered a halt and opened my door. "Cathcart. Let's go."

He was cool with that. Better to stick with the boss than wait in the car.

Moving toward the wire, we watched every step for anything even slightly not right. Reaching the cord, we checked the roadside mound, thirty meters to our right. Our trucks were about the same distance behind us. The storm to the north seemed to have blown away. Wispy clouds passed silently high above us.

We followed the wire with our eyes. Where it disappeared from view, I assumed it was buried. We walked beside it, maybe another twenty meters, and then it simply ended. As in, not buried and not connected to anything. Like the guy had unwound as much as he had, then ran to Home Depot to pick up another spool. Or maybe a battery. IEDs were sometimes assembled by different teams. One might emplace and bury the device, then another would come back with a battery and arming device, while a third might lie in wait to pull the trigger when their victims drove by. Maybe we had interrupted their setup process here.

Cathcart was likely thinking the same. "You think something scared him off, sir?"

"Maybe. I've never seen a loose end just left exposed."

"Want me to call EOD, sir?"

That was never anyone's first choice. Calling them meant we would be stuck out there another three or four hours, or as long as it took them to finish whatever devices they were already dismantling that day. And we only had a single Air Force EOD team for our entire battalion.

"Let's go back and see what he planted."

We hiked back toward the road, stopped maybe ten feet from the dirt mound. I was not concerned it would go off—the yellow cord clearly was not connected to a detonator. Peering over the mound, we both saw the wire indeed ran to a standard 155 mm howitzer shell. We could have blown it up ourselves with a blast from Brooks's .50, but a recovered IED offered a wealth of clues. How it was made and sometimes even who made it.

"It's dead, sir. Why don't we just pull it?"

That was an option. And yet something inside me recoiled. Call it intuition, or the heebie-jeebies, but this tiny voice somewhere warned me not to touch that wire. That was decision number two, and it probably saved all of us.

"Let's call EOD," I decided. "We'll keep four trucks here. The rest can head back."

"Roger that, sir."

Sighing, Cathcart took a knee and got on the horn. Sure, I had just killed the rest of our day, but I was not about to risk some other passing patrol getting killed for real.

With the report filed, we returned to our vehicles, and I briefed the two squads I picked to stay. Giving the rigged shell and that weird wire-to-nowhere a wide berth, we set up a security perimeter and steeled ourselves for the long, lonely wait.

Half a day later, two Air Force techs finally showed up. A severely overweight guy in charge, plus his helper. They unloaded and set up a Johnny Five—what we called their smaller, Wall-E–type robot on tank treads with a mechanical pincher arm and cameras. The tech plugged in the control module and sent the thing rolling out to examine our trap. Johnny Fives had mounted cameras that provided high-definition voyeurism, and we watched his dog-height point-of-view on a little video monitor. Just as it was getting close though, something happened. A tread went up on a rock or something, and the whole thing tipped over. Everybody deflated: another forty-five minutes down the drain. Fatso was glowering, like it was our fault he had broken his toy. Now he would have to put on a Michelin Man suit and waddle out there himself, grumble, grumble, grumble. Man, we could not stand those EOD people, but we had no clue that they would not only save our lives this time, but time and again.

Anyway, he finally got out there beside our death mound, got on his hands and knees, and poked around with a plastic prober. Minutes passed, everyone dreading some fatal mistake, but eventually he stood up again and waddled back to us, stopping only to put Wall-E back on his feet. When they got back to his vehicle, Cathcart and I were there waiting to hear his assessment.

"It's pretty bad," he explained. "Basically, what you see there is the tip of the iceberg. That shell is wired to four other shells buried all around it. If anybody tried to monkey with that setup, half this field would have gone up. You guys sure made the right call, Lieutenant."

Cathcart and I swallowed and surveyed the breadth of the kill zone with fresh eyes.

That is when it hit me: That highly visible yellow cord to nowhere had been set out as bait. It was meant to be noticed, meant to look useless, in hopes some impatient GI would do exactly as my man had suggested. The shudder that ran through me was twice as intense as the one that first warned me. The EOD tech explained that it was even worse than we thought. If we had pulled the cord, boom. If we had walked up to the bomb, boom. And if an EOD tech had tried to move the artillery round itself, there was a pressure activation device buried beneath it designed to detonate. It was not just a trap for us; it was a trap for the people trained to dismantle it.

And this fellow who saved our lives did not seem like such a jerk anymore. Yes, we initially scorned our EOD colleagues, but as the years went by, and the IEDs of Iraq grew increasingly lethal and prevalent, we came to regard those techs, along with our combat-engineer brothers who searched the millions of miles of roads for IEDs, as absolutely vital to our survival.

LESSON: INTUITION

Intuition is the ability to understand something immediately, without the need for conscious reasoning. In combat and in life I have felt this gut feeling many times, a very subtle sense that something was not right. Our brains are supercomputers taking in information in a depth we do not fully understand. We are doing pattern recognition, scanning for dangers even subconsciously, running on biological code that is ancient and hardwired.

A book I greatly admire is Gavin de Becker's *The Gift of Fear*, which explains that intuition is a crucial survival tool. It predicts and prevents violence by processing subtle, often ignored, pre-incident indicators. De Becker teaches how to recognize these survival signals, trust gut feelings, understand how predators manipulate, and take protective action to avoid danger. Intuition often provides accurate warnings long before a threat becomes obvious.

This story provided two clear moments of intuition. The first was the small, quiet voice that told me to stop at the stranded vehicle with the family, a warning I overrode in the name of the schedule. The second was the gut feeling not to pull that bright-yellow wire. One ignored, one followed. The difference was life and death.

Listening to your gut is not just about surviving firefights or roadside bombs. That voice in your head may whisper at times when the stakes seem much smaller. It may tell you that something is off in a business deal, that a relationship is not what it seems, that your child needs you to slow down and pay attention. It may not always be life or death, but that does not make it less important. The habit of listening to that voice, of at least stopping and considering what it is trying to tell you, is vital in any field.

After many close calls, I have learned to treat that inner voice with respect. It does not mean you stop every time or that instinct replaces logic. But when it speaks, you would be a fool to ignore it.

Intuition is not magic. It is your mind and body working together to recognize patterns and signals you might not even consciously process. And it might just be the difference between walking into disaster and finding a better way forward.

CHAPTER 5

THE RAITA

THE CHHATRAPATI SHIVAJI TERMINUS IN Mumbai isn't one of the Eight Wonders of the World, but it could be. Known locally as CST, it is a majestic Gothic palace of a train station, with a dizzying mishmash of Romanesque, baroque, and Indian architectural accents. The only thing busier than its myriad facades, arches, towers, and spires is all the foot traffic, with three million commuters per day jostling their way to and from the eighteen major railway platforms. Approaching via the thronging broad avenue, entering the main doors beneath the clock tower, and ascending the grand stairway is like stepping back into the heart of the British Old Empire.

Sadly, in this century, CST was also the scene of a horrific massacre.

On November 26, 2008, two Pakistani terrorists dressed as tourists casually walked in and began randomly killing people with AK-47s and grenades. India refers to that day as 26/11, their own shattering equivalent of 9/11. A total of ten armed terrorists from the Pakistan-based group Lashkar-e-Taiba (LeT) launched coordinated attacks on five sites across Mumbai, near simultaneously, including hotels, a train station, a Jewish center, and a café. Just ten men were able to bring a megacity of more than eighteen million people to its knees. The siege lasted approximately sixty hours before Indian security forces regained control and killed or captured all attackers.

"The killers knew their target well," I explained to our group. "An easily accessible public space, tightly packed with civilians who had limited avenues of escape. It was the perfect kill zone."

As with America's own atrocity, police and defense experts have an obligation to weigh every factor of what went right and wrong that day and share that wisdom with the coming generations of freedom's defenders. In the decade following my retirement from the Army, I became one of those experts. A master's degree from Georgetown led to a job at the Pentagon, then a faculty post at West Point, the Army's elite officer academy. Never much for book learning as a kid, I was surprised by how much I enjoyed teaching, whether in the classroom sharing the wisdom of Sun Tzu, Clausewitz, and Thucydides, or in the field. One of the academy's best programs sends selected cadets abroad to study modern-day hot spots like Bosnia, Sri Lanka, Ukraine, and Georgia. In 2018 the destination was India, and I was one of the faculty chosen to accompany ten of our finest future officers to the world's most populous democracy.

For most of the two-week schedule, I was a supporting instructor for the cadets' guided study of India's defense and foreign policy issues. But for three days in Mumbai, I was the lead teacher, guiding our delegation through the complexities of the city and the horrors of 26/11 to illustrate the lessons of urban warfare.

I bring a certain flair to the classroom, but keeping eyes on me in India proved a challenge, the primary distraction being the assault on Western sensibilities that is Mumbai itself. The five-hundred-year-old heart of a region of twenty-three million people, it seethes and overspills with a densely packed, ever-circulating blend of a thousand subcultures that often strikes newcomers as total anarchy. There is ostentatious wealth, grinding poverty, and every standard of living between, all on a scale that dwarfs the biggest American metropolises. Walking the streets is a sensory bombardment, and CST, their Grand Central Station, crams all this human energy into an even tighter package. Trains roll in and out, passengers filling every possible space—hanging off the sides, even riding up top, and leaping off as the brakes screech.

Surveying our wide-eyed cadets, I thought of myself at seventeen, similarly awestruck as my Humvee sped across Panama City. I had come a long way in twenty-five years, traveled the world over for my research, but Mumbai was beyond anything I had experienced as well. It was the faces of the *Slumdog* kids that really got to me, these armies of the neglected. I was a dad myself now, with three little ones back in Colorado, and this trip had interrupted my new role as Mr. Mom.

We also visited Dharavi, one of the world's largest slums, squeezed into less than a single square mile yet home to nearly a million souls. Its narrow lanes and improvised dwellings seemed to stretch endlessly, the density almost unimaginable. The cadets had read about poverty in books, but walking those passages, seeing children playing barefoot in alleys where open sewers ran, families crowded into tin-roofed rooms smaller than a cadet's dorm, and entire neighborhoods built of scrap wood and sheet metal, shook many of them in a way no classroom lesson ever could. Some cadets were quiet for hours afterward. For future officers, raised on the order and structure of West Point, the chaos and resilience of Dharavi left a lasting imprint, a reminder of the human conditions wars are often fought within and around.

Work is work, I thought, as I raised my voice above the din. "The terrorists struck around 2130 hours, in a rampage that lasted ninety minutes. Countless lives were saved when a station announcer calmly advised the crowd to evacuate, but it took the authorities over an hour to enter the station in sufficient force. The killers fled before them but left fifty-eight dead and over a hundred wounded."

It was a grim feeling, standing on the very floor where it unfolded, fingering the bullet holes left in the concrete pillars, studying the obsidian memorial shrine, replaying the scene in our collective mind's eye. Nor did the horror end at the CST. The two Pakistanis dashed on foot toward a local hospital, where they fatally ambushed a car full of high-ranking counterterrorism officials. As we stood staring at the last pavement those cops ever saw, I motioned for Cadet Brandon Driscoll to take the floor.

One of the quieter ones, he seemed unsure of how to begin. Finally, he looked up. "My name is Arun Jadhav," he told us in a strong, clear voice. "In 2008 I had been a police officer for twenty years. That morning, I had been chasing down a gangster. Then I got the call that a rampage was in progress, and they assigned me to a protection detail."

No, Driscoll was not hallucinating. He was completing one of the best assignments the academy has developed for understanding warfare, as well as a favorite technique of mine: the staff ride. It requires homework. I announce in class which battle we will study, then assign each student the role of an individual who was actually there. You study everything your "character" did that day, their background and life, consider the decisions they made, and the context of those moments. Then, as we walk the actual ground, each student plays their part. They speak from the point of view of the person they studied, and thus we all educate each other in a far more immediate, visceral way than you could ever get from a history book.

Constable Arun Jadhav's story was chilling. As Cadet Driscoll explained, he was one of seven men riding in the police command vehicle when the two CST terrorists jumped out and raked them at close range with machine-gun fire. In the firefight that followed, Jadhav managed to wound one terrorist before getting shot twice. Around him, five of his colleagues were dead, with the sixth barely breathing. "They pulled three bodies out and dumped them on the street," Driscoll told us, his voice cracking. "Then they climbed in the car and drove off. They thought all four of us in back were dead. I tried to raise my rifle, but my wounds made it impossible. When the constable next to me moaned, one of the terrorists turned and shot him dead. I had no doubt I was going to die back there as well."

Miraculously, he did not. The terrorists soon fled the car, and the chase on the streets continued until they ran into a police blockade. In the shootout there, one terrorist was finally killed, and the man Constable Jadhav wounded was captured. When Cadet Driscoll finished his report, we gave him a round of applause. He had managed to include details I had not known, which to me is the mark of a successful staff ride.

Unfortunately, our group was taking casualties as well. No one was getting shot, but this enemy was always close and struck without warning. I know what you are thinking: bees. But no. This time it was food-and-water-borne bacterial infections, the most common ailment for Westerners visiting Asia. In India, they call it "Delhi belly."

Having served in rural Iraq, the tenets of safe consumption were deeply ingrained in me. Do not drink the local tap water or brush your teeth with it. Do not even look at their water unless it comes in a sealed bottle or you actually see it being boiled. Only accept hot tea from a local, never soda. Everyone from West Point had been briefed, as well as dosed with a slew of vaccines before we departed. But until you have seen, and smelled, dysentery, it is easy to slip up and do one of the zillion things Americans routinely do with food, drink, or water without a second thought.

It took about three days in India for our first cadet to go down. Cadet Smithfield, a big-hearted football hero from Chattanooga, came down to breakfast pale and sweating. Two hours later, he was back in bed, moaning with fever, chills, vomiting, and diarrhea. We did not see him for three days, and he missed our day in Kashmir. A day later, Boone fell out. Then two more, with Captain Myrick the first instructor to succumb. I kept my eyes peeled for careless moves and intervened when I could—like confiscating a generously offered bottle of Coke. "I know that cap feels tight, cadet, but it is probably a refilled bottle. They do not just throw stuff away in these countries." Unfortunately, I could not watch them all twenty-four seven.

Following the train station, our Tragical History Tour continued at Nariman House, a five-story complex in a working-class area of old Mumbai. It was part of the Chabad House network of Jewish cultural centers and another site of a 26/11 attack. The men who hit the CST were not the only killers on a rampage that day. Just as al-Qaeda split into small teams to hijack four US airliners on 9/11, the Pakistani terrorists launched simultaneous attacks at multiple locations across Mumbai. It is a key tactic for the agents of chaos, as the hundreds of incoming cell phone calls from traumatized witnesses quickly overwhelm emergency response systems and sow confusion between overlapping authorities.

As the slaughter began at the station, two other terrorists broke into Nariman House. They took six hostages, including the young director—Brooklyn-born Rabbi Gavriel Holtzberg—and his pregnant Israeli wife, Rivka, both revered for their humanitarian outreach. Authorities quickly surrounded the complex, but the terrorists held them at bay, stalling and negotiating by phone even as they bound, tortured, and killed some of their prisoners. Just before dawn, Indian commandos stormed the place. In the cat-and-mouse battle that lasted most of the day, all the remaining hostages, both terrorists, and one Indian soldier lost their lives.

Standing next to the building where the Indian forces had rappelled down from helicopters, I pointed out the nightmare zoning of the surrounding neighborhood. "You have solid concrete walls on all four sides of this place, and the street out front is less than a lane wide, so it is impossible to surround. Police procedure was to seal the location for the counterterrorism unit, only they happened to be tied up in New Delhi."

So if you are keeping score: Two men hit the CST. Two more took the Jewish center.

Unfortunately, that was not even the half of it.

There were five Pakistani hit teams sent to wreak havoc across Mumbai that fateful day. Ten men had carefully studied the places they attacked, knew exactly where to go, at what time, and carried weapons best suited to killing as many innocent people as possible. Some of the ten killers died themselves that day. Others took hostages and cheated death for the next three days. Unfortunately for the mystery planners, financiers, and trainers of the operation, one terrorist was taken alive. It was the second man from the train station, the one wounded by Constable Jadhav. Such fanatics often prove impervious to interrogation and take their secrets to the grave.

Not this guy. He was proud of what he had done. And happy to talk about it.

He and his nine partners were all Pakistani twentysomethings of meager means. Their minds filled by years of anti-Hindu, anti-Indian, and anti-Semitic propaganda, agents of LeT recognized their malleability, recruited them with promises of cash payments to their families upon their deaths, and trained them to unleash hell on the cosmopolitan heart of the neighboring nation they despised. LeT further enjoyed an advantage most terrorists can only dream of: the backing of a powerful faction inside Pakistan's military intelligence service, the ISI.

The ISI did not just train and equip the marauders. They were monitoring and advising them in real time throughout the three days of attacks, and the man in the hospital spilled it all: names, dates, places. Unlike 9/11, 26/11 was an act of war by a hostile government, Pakistan being India's eternal foe. Both countries possess nuclear weapons, and each has sworn the other's destruction. In 2008 it was not hard to see the fallout spinning toward doomsday.

Officially, of course, Pakistan was outraged, just as they were three years later when American SEALs killed Osama bin Laden in an al-Qaeda safe house. After the world heard everything the Mumbai killer had to say, the Pakistani government swore to render all due assistance in bringing his coconspirators to justice.

They did nothing of the kind. The only man sent to the gallows was the blabbermouth.

We had three days left in India, with our final stay in New Delhi.

Health wise, I was the last man standing. Well, outside of Colonel Liam Collins, who seemed barely human in his ability to keep going. More about him later. One by one, every cadet and faculty member had taken ill. Everyone had missed at least one day of the program. Overall, I had enjoyed the trip, the whirling kaleidoscope of this vast, new land, but I was hitting my cultural saturation point too. And a world away, three little Spencers were missing their daddy as much as I missed them.

A little after breakfast, I was upstairs gathering what I needed for the day when I felt the first twinge of stomach upset. It could not be from what I had just eaten: idli, essentially steamed rice cakes topped by sambar, a cooked vegetable stew, and my chai had been piping hot. I felt my guts churn more sharply, then that first queasy pang of needing to relieve myself.

Time ticked by in the bathroom. I texted the director, said I would be a few minutes late.

At some point in there, it hit me: the raita.

It is a ubiquitous Indian side dish and palate cleanser, made from yogurt, cream, and mild spices. What else is usually part of the recipe? Thin slices of fresh tomato and cucumber. Fresh vegetables, which I now suspected somebody had washed in local tap water.

There was nobody to blame. I knew my enemy yet had spooned him into my mouth all the same. It was only a finger bowl of raita, though. Maybe my tummy ache would pass.

Two hours later, I was writhing feverishly in soaked sheets.

Everybody else on this long, strange trip had taken this ride, and now it was my turn. The next two days passed in a blur. Staring up at the ceiling or down into cold white porcelain. I missed our cultural side trip to the Taj Mahal, our only day to forget terrorism and be tourists.

Thankfully, by Day 3, all the Imodium and antibiotics seemed to be turning the tide, which was lucky because come evening we would all be on that big bird back home. The worst of my symptoms had passed, which merely left me feeling like I had been hit by a truck. Hopefully, my twenty-five-plus hours in the air back to Colorado would largely pass with me in slumberland.

I took a little chicken soup on our last Indian restaurant visit and managed to keep it down, my first sustenance and fluid. Looking in the mirror, I saw a pale, wracked version of myself and resolved to rest as much as possible. If I came home looking like death warmed over, my kids would freak.

And then about an hour before the bus was due to take us to the airport, my Delhi belly re-erupted, and there I was again in my temporary quarters on the bathroom floor.

It seemed impossible. I had been getting better. Slowly, but definitely. None of my students or colleagues had suffered a relapse, so what the hell was going on? And more importantly, how was I going to get out of the country? They were not going to hold the plane for me.

I lost more fluids over the next hour than I could have possibly had inside me. And, between bouts of agony, I managed to cram my belongings into my luggage. All the while, the big hand on the clock kept ticking toward go time. I would have to expel as much as I possibly could at the very precipice, then find my footing and make it down to the lobby before the next wave hit. Maybe a ten-minute window. It was going to be close. And please, please, let there be a commode on that bus.

Faces swiveled expectantly as I walked gingerly across the grand reception area. "Morning, sir. You feeling OK?"

"Mm-hm." Trying not to move any facial muscles. Praying nobody jostled me.

I made it onto the bus. Walked all the way to the back, grabbed the seat beside the thin water closet door. Which I used a time or two on the way, but I arrived at the airport upright, dabbing sweat off my face with a damp paper towel.

Three more hurdles to go. Customs. Security. Boarding.

Any inkling of my true condition at these check-ins, and they would have grounded me in a heartbeat.

I hit the restroom prior to each. Splashed water on my face, combed my hair, rehearsed a smile.

"I trust you enjoyed your stay in our country, Sahib?"

"Mm-hm."

"Are you feeling all right, sir?"

"Never better."

I was pretty sure whatever microbes swimming inside me were worse than Delhi belly. I needed a hospital, and I definitely wanted one located on American soil. It was sixteen hours to New York. If I could just get in the air, people would tolerate a guy being sick. I just could not pass out, especially over Europe, or they would land somewhere and shove me out the door.

I fooled 'em all, I thought as I stepped into the jetway. Only it was stifling hot in there. We stood crammed in a line, mere steps away from the door.

Oh, no. Not here. Please, not here.

Immediately on boarding, I dove for the restroom.

Ten minutes later, my next challenge: I had been assigned a middle seat. That was not going to work. As subtly as possible, I started asking people to trade. Big surprise: Nobody wants to circumvent the globe in a middle seat. Blinking in near delirium, I tried to sweeten the deal. "Hundred bucks, folks. Who is going to take this nice, crisp, American C-note for an aisle seat?"

I went up to four hundred and was about to go to five when a senior colleague finally took pity on me. And his seat was right next to the bathroom. Finally, some relief from the universe.

What followed was the longest, most agonizing, genuinely frightening sixteen hours of my life, at least half of which I spent literally diving in and out of that little plastic restroom.

Twelve hours to New York. "Oh, no snacks. Thank you."

"Coffee? Tea? Bottled water?"

I shook my head. Six hours to go.

My breathing slowed; my pulse felt weak. I am not a doctor, but I knew my insides were starting to liquefy. You are losing more than your body can take. People in my condition suffer organ failure. People can die. I definitely felt like I was on track.

Two hours to go. Still conscious, at least. The stink of me emanating. So many concerned looks.

I went straight to urgent care in New York City. They hooked me to an IV, hard to find a vein due to dehydration, and pumped me full of everything. I immediately took in three bags of fluids. The doctor at the urgent care's best guess as to what I had? Food poisoning.

And the most likely culprit had to be that chicken soup. The last thing I had eaten in India, hoping to strengthen myself for the flight.

But the urgent care crew did not have time to really explore or run any tests. I had to catch a flight to Colorado Springs in a few hours. I was also supposed to pick up my kids. My wife was deployed overseas, so my sister had been staying at our place, but she had to go. Scrambling, I called my few close friends in Colorado. Dan and his wife told me not to worry, said their own kids would love having the company.

Exhaling, I told urgent care I had to go and catch the next flight I could grab.

Which proved to be another mistake, but so it goes.

They told me if I did not improve, go straight to the hospital.

When I finally unlocked the door to my house in Colorado Springs, I knew I had to lie down for a few minutes before I did anything else. But I was still in bad shape and needed a doctor. So I dropped my bag and headed straight to the hospital. Their best guess was not food poisoning, since I was not getting any better, but C. diff (or *Clostridioides difficile* infection) from taking too many antibiotics (something I had not stopped since I first got sick). They gave me more antibiotics, supposedly special ones. Once I finally made it back through the door of my house to lie down, I did not get up for four days.

Dan, a saint in my eyes by this point, kept checking in on me and kept me well-stocked with probiotic yogurt, Gatorade, and meds. "Just bring the kids back," I finally rasped. "I cannot be alone anymore."

He did. They came bounding in. Isaac was seven. We high-fived, like men. Daughter Isabel, five, the caretaker, laid a concerned palm on my forehead. "Are you OK, Daddy?" Frowning, she about-faced and marched back out, while Maggie, three, snuggled in beside me.

Isabel returned with her Doc McStuffins medical kit. Up went the lid, out came a little blue mallet. You know, so she could check my reflexes.

I had returned to an empty house, but now, finally, I was home.

LESSON: PERSPECTIVE

If there is one thing I have learned in my life and career, from leaving a small town in Indiana to serving across the globe, it is the power of perspective. Mumbai was a master class in it. The city's scale alone was overwhelming, but standing on the ground where terrorists slaughtered innocent civilians, walking through the narrow lanes of Dharavi where a million people live in conditions below what most Americans can imagine, and watching cadets experience it all for the first time, reminded me how much of life and war comes down to perspective.

The staff ride itself is designed to provide exactly that. It forces cadets to put themselves in another person's shoes, to see decisions made in the chaos of the moment, and to understand context that cannot be captured in a textbook. Mumbai gave them another layer of perspective altogether: the raw confrontation with poverty, violence, and resilience in a way no classroom could provide.

Perspective is not just for cadets. It has been my pursuit throughout my life. Leaving the quiet suburbs of Indiana for Panama, Italy, Iraq, and every corner of the world I have walked since, I have sought perspective. It is what I want most to give my children as they grow, helping them see their lives and their challenges in the broader frame of the world. And it is what I try to offer others through my research, bringing back fragments of perspective from war zones so that lessons can be understood—not as abstractions but as lived human experience.

In the military, we had a saying: It could always be worse. You learn that in training as much as in war. Whether you are soaking wet, freezing cold, hungry, or bone tired, perspective is what allows you to keep moving. Even in our most elite schools, like Ranger School, the point is not just to push soldiers to their physical limits, but to give them perspective—so that later, when life or combat feels unbearable, they know they can endure.

Perspective teaches humility. It teaches gratitude. It reminds us that what feels hard often is not and that others have endured far worse. Even when I feel like something is not going right, or my goals are not being met, perspective reminds me of what truly matters. As a parent, it means putting myself in my children's shoes, remembering how small their world is and how big their problems feel to them. As a leader, it means stepping into the shoes of those I serve and teach. And as a boss, gaining the perspective of an employee is just as valuable—because leadership is not only about giving direction. It is about understanding the people you are leading.

The goal, for me, has always been to keep gaining perspective, to pass it on to my children, and to share it with others. Because in war, in research, in leadership, in parenting, and in life, perspective changes everything.

CHAPTER 6

PEPPER

IT'S BEEN FUN DIPPING BACK into the various stages of my life and career.

Platoon leader. War researcher. West Point instructor. Husband and father.

Had anyone told me at seventeen I'd one day hold any of these positions, I would have laughed. The only thing I wanted to be when I grew up was a high-speed, low-drag, fired-up, Captain America super soldier in an elite unit of the US Army. A doer of daring, a brother-in-arms, a red-blooded, all-American hero.

At age nineteen, two years into my service, all my dreams came true when I was assigned to the 2nd Battalion, 75th Ranger Regiment at Fort Lewis, Washington. At long last I was one of them, the Best of the Best, and I was thrilled by that truth every waking moment. There were older guys in the unit who went home to wives and children, but all of us still young and unmarried were inseparable. Night and day, we trained together, ate together, and lived four to a room. Off duty, we stayed together as well. The bond was tribal in the best sense, far beyond what you would find in a fraternity or club, because it was built on the knowledge that one day each of us might have to put another's life above our own, to step in front of the bullet meant for him. Being willing to die for the other guy wasn't just a platitude in this group. It was the whole point.

The three defining pillars of our existence were embodied in the Ranger Creed, which we recited and lived daily. "I will uphold the prestige, honor, and high esprit de corps of my Ranger Regiment," proclaims the opening stanza. We knew that meant we should conduct ourselves with the highest professionalism, with the reputation of a Ranger and the Regiment always in mind. To young men, of course, it also means, "Nobody messes with us."

And one day, it came to pass that somebody did mess with us. With me, specifically.

How did I respond?

By opening a big ol' can of whoop-ass. Like, full Charles Bronson.

It was pure instinct and the only thing that made sense to me at the time. The end result was bodily injury—and, worse, getting dropped from the only tribe I ever aspired to join, the only place in the world I'd ever wanted to be. So take note, young warriors. This is how you win the fight but lose what really matters.

It started, as these things often do, at a local watering hole. This one was called Cowboys. It was about forty-five minutes from Fort Lewis, but we made the drive because it was all ages, and we weren't old enough to drink. The other big draw was the line dancing and all the fine wannabe cowgirls in sprayed-on jeans and shimmery tube tops who came to strut their stuff. The place smelled like cigarettes, leather boots, and desperation.

As soldier boys with high-and-tight haircuts, we stuck out like sore thumbs, but we never had much trouble. If anything, the locals were often downright solicitous to us out-of-towners, and invitations to their after-hours, middle-of-nowhere bonfires were common. I don't know how many of us got lucky, but it was cool listening to music and laughs with flannel-and-denim-clad twenty-somethings who weren't all that different from the kids I grew up with back in Indiana.

On the night in question, my buddy Kent and I accepted such an invite. He'd been talking boar hunting with some guy, and the hunter's girlfriend had this cute, single friend. She had this great laugh and told us to just call her Zima Spice. When Zima decided we needed to bounce out to "the quarry," Kent and I were all in.

Maybe a fifteen-minute drive later, the five of us hooked up with a few dozen backwoods burner types gabbing around a campfire. A half keg wrapped in burlap, a paint-flecked boombox blasting Garth Brooks. Sparks popped, smoke stung my eyes, and shadows leapt across faces in the firelight. Kent was busy talking hog dogs with his new pal, and I was making headway with Zima. She and this other girl were kind of digging my paratrooper rap: "The beauty of a moonless night jump is you have no idea where you are. Could be five seconds 'til you hit the ground, maybe a minute. All you can do is relax and enjoy the ride. Cool wind in your face, stars up in the sky. It's as close as a soldier gets to pure bliss."

And then blackness.

Next thing, I was coming to, skull throbbing like a jackhammer, and I realized a bunch of guys were dragging me. Still groggy, desperately trying to figure out what happened, I rolled my neck and saw one of the people hauling me was Kent. Only it was hard to recognize him because his face and clothes were a mess of blood.

Maybe I blacked out again because what I next remember is being back at our Ford Ranger hearing, "You guys need to get out of here." But the more I came to, the more questions I had.

"Dude, what happened?"

Apparently one of the burners had taken issue with my gentle wooing of the fair maidens. Supposedly, he yelled across the fire at me to cool it, only I didn't hear it over the blaring music, so he took a baseball bat and smacked a homer off the base of my skull. Kent flipped out when he saw it. He grabbed the guy, which proved a mistake because the burner's buddies immediately jumped him. Kent went to the ground, and they proceeded to beat the spit out of him. I pictured him curled in the dirt with boots hammering into him, ribs cracking, the crowd cheering like it was Friday night entertainment.

The boar hunter finally stopped it. Grabbed some of his buddies, and they dragged/carried/hustled us out of there, leaving the score Burners 2, Rangers 0.

I only had one question. "Which guy was it?"

Kent shook his head. "Could be Pepper. Some dude kept yelling, "Yo, Pepper!"

The docs at the emergency room at Fort Lewis patched us up. For me that meant stitches in my head and the ceremonial Motrin that I had already learned was the quintessential Army remedy to all ailments, no matter the severity (well, almost). Take 800 milligrams, drink water, come back later. Bar fights being their bread and butter, they only asked a few questions, which we brushed off with vague murmurs, and they cut us loose without making a stink.

Back in the barracks, the story spread fast. It was impossible not to talk about it. I must have told the story ten times that afternoon, and every time it picked up more edge, more detail, more anger. Every Ranger who heard it reacted the same way. *How dare they.* Imagine twenty teenage Rangers furious that anyone had the audacity to defile the honor of the Regiment. It was not just an insult to me but an insult to all of us, to the Rangers, to the Army itself. The barracks filled with talk of payback. Plans started forming almost on their own. "We have to get them." That phrase was repeated like a battle cry. Boots stomped, fists slammed into palms, dip spit hit the barracks trash cans as pacing men muttered about revenge.

Inside my own head, I was conflicted. I wanted nothing to do with more fighting, but I felt I had to go along with it. I felt the pull of justice for the disrespect to me, to the Rangers, to the Army. I had already been stitched up once that day, and I knew how fast things could spiral. But another part of me felt trapped by the weight of expectation, by the unspoken rule that you did not walk away when the Regiment's honor was at stake. Justice, or at least the Ranger version of it, demanded action.

By the time the sun set, the decision was made. Probably six hours later, me and fifteen of my closest Ranger buddies were back on the road.

In Cowboys's parking lot, I had two guys follow me in, motioned the rest to hang tight.

As I said, soldier boys stood out in that place. It was like all the line dancing stopped, the bartenders froze mid-pour, and patrons went wide-eyed. Somewhere, a lonely harmonica wailed.

"I'm lookin' for Pepper," I growled.

A pair of muttonchops sidled up to me. "Pepper says he'll meet you. In the alley, back of the club. Don't bring your friends or we'll bring ours."

I walked out of the club and headed back to my fellow Rangers, and we all walked down the street to the alley like a scene from the movie *Reservoir Dogs*. Boots struck pavement in sync, shoulders squared, eyes hard. The kind of walk that dared anyone to get in the way.

The alley was not far, so it wasn't hard to find the OK Corral, especially as a crowd of about fifty had already gathered. Again, I swaggered in with my crew. The locals parted, leaving a solitary dude as my challenger.

He didn't look like much. Maybe twenty or twenty-one, but grizzled and wild-eyed. Average height, average build, Judas Priest T-shirt. I knew I could take him. One of my buddies grabbed my head, told me to take off my shirt. I assume this was a primal attempt to signal physical dominance.

"You're Pepper?"

He made no reply. Just came at me, swinging.

OK, let's stop here for a minute and talk a little about my fighting skills. I mean, you may be thinking, *Ha! With all of John's training, that doofus didn't stand a chance!*

Yeah, here's the thing, though. We never actually trained for hand-to-hand combat.

What? Dude, you knew how to kill people! Weren't you a lean, mean, fighting machine?

Well, yes and no. Sure, I could've dropped him at three hundred meters with an M4 rifle. Shredded him with a Claymore mine, impaled him with a bayonet. Fists, though? Not so much.

Huh. So I guess you were all badass before you joined the Army?

Uh, no. My only fight in high school was when Dooby Don Gorman slammed my head into my locker. Before I could even turn around, kids were jumping in to keep us apart, which is probably what Dooby was counting on. I mean, does that even count as a fight?

C'mon, John. Don't Army guys have to bash each other with those big, padded sticks?

Pugil sticks. Yeah, we did those. But guess what nobody bothers to explain before the fight? How to actually use a pugil stick. The whole idea is just to make you face fear. You get to find out what it feels like to take a hit, even if it is through a helmet and from a giant padded stick that looks like a cotton swab on steroids. There is no real skill transfer. Nobody ever shows you the right way to swing one. It is nothing more than a glorified shoving match, an exercise in aggression with the danger turned way down.

So you were all Army Rangers, and none of you were trained in hand-to-hand combat?

Again, yes and no. The Army had dropped boxing as pointless on the modern battlefield, but the Ranger high brass knew we needed real hand-to-hand skills. What we had on the books then was the old bayonet training, where you practiced thrusts and parries into a padded dummy while yelling out loud on a scripted course. It was comical at best, especially in the age of rifles, night vision, and body armor. The Ranger brass, LTC, and later four-star General Stanley McChrystal sent one of our senior sergeants around the world to study the best fighting styles, including the Gracie school in California. At the same time, Ultimate Fighting was exploding in popularity. We even ended up hosting Brazil's famed Gracie brothers as guest instructors. By the time Pepper came swinging for me that night, I had maybe four lessons under my belt.

That is not to scoff at those four lessons. The senior sergeant sent around the world had brought back a raw form of hand to hand that we tested in the most primal way: the circle of death. We would form two circles, an outer and an inner, standing about two arms' lengths apart, so each man faced an opponent directly in front of him. At the whistle, the fight began. You went one-on-one until someone quit or blacked out. There were no punches, only violent throws, bone-rattling takedowns, and the new chokes and arm bars we were trying to master at a breakneck pace. After about ten minutes, another whistle would blow, and the inner circle rotated, giving you a new opponent. No rest, no escape. Just sweat, fear, and the knowledge that the next man might be stronger, meaner, or more skilled than the one before.

We did not realize it then, but we were at the ground floor of what would become the Army's new hand-to-hand system. This was not the pugil stick circle of stupidity. It was a crucible where you learned to face the fear of being strangled, slammed into the ground, or bent until your joints screamed. Worst of all, it was where you risked being viewed or taken as a coward in front of your brothers. And yet you had to move forward through pain, panic, and humiliation, learning how to fight with control, to push someone to their limit without crippling them, to give everything without crossing the line that broke the bond.

Still, four lessons leave you with almost nothing. At best, you survived a few more seconds longer than someone who knew nothing at all. All I really carried into that night was the barest sense of how to close the distance and not stand frozen while someone punched, stabbed, or shot me at close range.

So what were you thinking as you strode through that crowd? What was your strategy?

None. Zero. The only thought in my head was avenging my honor. Upholding that Ranger Creed in front of my brothers. This is why young men fight. Their brains are developmentally lacking in risk assessment. We are primed to rush headlong to our doom. I was probably thinking of my mom as well. When my sister told her that Dooby hit me, she stared me down and said, "You better kick that kid's ass. Or I'll kick yours." And she wasn't being funny.

As far as jiujitsu went, all I knew was not to swing at an experienced swinger. Instead, I closed the distance. Got inside Pepper's reach, grappled him, then dragged and threw his ass to the pavement. The impact rattled my bones.

Realizing he couldn't Mike Tyson me in a boxing duel, the dude went nuts, his hands beating and clawing at me for any advantage. His fingernails raked my skin. His thumbs pressed into my eyeballs with enough force to make white sparks explode in my vision. I knew enough to maintain my position on top of him, my weight pressing down, but we rolled, literally into the sodden gutter. The stench hit me immediately, a rank stew of oil and mildew, cigarette butts floating in black water that soaked into my pants. The crowd whooped and hollered, a storm of voices bouncing off the brick walls, boots stomping, fists pumping in the air. My heart hammered. How close my own boys were, I couldn't tell.

Then came the moment that changed everything. Our two faces mashed together, breath hot, sweat and grime smeared between us. Pepper's mouth opened wide and clamped down on the side of my head. Pain like fire tore through me. It was not a nip. It was a savage tearing, cartilage crunching, blood spraying across his face. My ear. My blood ran down my neck, warm and slick. The world narrowed to red pain.

I fought back on instinct. I threw my arm around his neck, twisted, and jerked him back into a reverse guillotine. My forearm crushed his windpipe, the back of his head locked to my chest. He bellowed like a calf on branding day, thrashing, spit flying, body jerking like he was being electrocuted. I just squeezed harder. His veins bulged against my arm. His nails dug furrows into my skin.

The crowd's mood shifted. The whoops turned into shrieks. "Yo, let him up!" "He's done!" "You're gonna kill him!" The words barely pierced the haze. All I felt was rage, my ear on fire, blood dripping off my chin. Seconds stretched like minutes.

Finally, I loosened. Pepper sagged limp. I shoved him off and reached up. My hand came away soaked, hot with blood.

Then, like a soundtrack, the rising wail of sirens. Red and blue lights strobed against the alley walls. The crowd scattered like a pack of rats. My brothers surged in, grabbing me, shoving my shirt against the wound. "Your ear looks bad, but we have to go!"

They dragged me to the car. We peeled out one end of the alley as the cops skidded in the other.

As my buddy's car sped down the highway, faster than the situation required, I pulled down the visor to check the damage. There wasn't much to inspect. Half my ear was gone. Pepper had Mike Tysoned me before Tyson ever touched Holyfield. For the rest of my life people would bring that up.

I wound up seeing the same docs in the emergency room at Fort Lewis that I had seen less than twenty-four hours earlier, only this injury was way more interesting than a near concussion. Pepper had bitten deep, and no animal bite contains more potentially deadly bacteria than a human's. They zapped me with antibiotics, coagulants to staunch the bleeding. Then came the scrub. A nurse rolled up with a stainless-steel tray and a brush that looked like it belonged at a hardware store. They dunked it in antiseptic and started scrubbing the ragged edge of what was left of my ear.

People ask me if it hurt when Pepper bit it off. I usually tell them no, that the adrenaline masked it. But I felt every bristle of that brush. Each stroke was like fire on raw nerves. My teeth ground together until my jaw ached. My hands clawed at the bed rails. Sweat poured down my face. My vision blurred. The pain was worse than the fight itself, worse than the bite, worse than anything I had felt in my life.

Next came a bandage that felt like seaweed under gauze, but not before every med tech on duty cycled through to gawk at the damage. Some laughed nervously, some winced, others debated my options out loud, as if I were not sitting there bleeding on the table.

Polaroids snapped. Word had spread across the hospital. A Ranger had gotten his ear bitten off in a backwoods alley fight.

And then the MPs showed up. Boots on tile, clipboards in hand, they wanted the whole story. Like an idiot, I gave it to them. Every detail, from Cowboys to the alley to Pepper's teeth. I told it like it was something to be proud of, like a war story. Their pens scratched furiously, and every line they wrote was another nail in the coffin of my Ranger career.

Later, the surgeons laid out their plan. I needed reconstructive surgery. They wanted to pull cartilage from my ribs or somewhere else on my body to rebuild what I had lost. But here was the catch. Surgery meant being put on medical profile. And in the Rangers, a profile meant you were out. Someone else would get your slot. And once gone, good luck ever getting it back. There were hundreds of soldiers desperate for a chance to wear the scroll and tan beret, waiting like wolves to take the place of anyone who faltered.

For me, it wasn't really a choice. I would have loved a shiny new ear, but I loved being a Ranger more. So I refused. I stuck with the seaweed compresses, ripping them off every few days, smearing on ointment while my exposed cartilage slowly scabbed and healed. It was disgusting, it hurt like hell, and it left me with a deformity that strangers now assume is a birth defect. But it kept me in the fight. Or so I thought.

And before you ask, no, I had not been drinking at any point in this story. Not only was I and everyone involved not of drinking age (that's not to say the civilians might not have been drinking), but I never picked it up. Not once in my entire time in the military. I always find it amusing that people are more surprised by that than by the fact I had my ear bitten off.

In the end, my tough-it-out approach didn't save me. My battalion commander or command sergeant major never yelled, never berated me. They didn't need to. They just signed the paperwork. Reassigned, for medical reasons. Apply to return when healthy. That was it. I was out of the Regiment. I had walked into that office a Ranger and walked out an exile. No ceremony, no last formation, no chance to prove myself again. Just a signature on a piece of paper that felt like a death sentence.

And where was I sent? The 25th Infantry Division. Regular Army. Their barracks happened to sit right on the other side of a chain-link fence from the Rangers. It was like being banished from your tribe but forced to live within sight of the fire. I could smell the gun oil, hear the laughter, feel the rhythm of their life continuing without me.

At seventeen, I wanted nothing more than to be Captain America, a super soldier among the Best of the Best. For one brief moment I had it. For one brief moment I wore the scroll, stood shoulder to shoulder with the tribe I had dreamed about since I was a boy. And then it was gone. Not lost on some battlefield halfway around the world, but in a muddy alley behind a honky-tonk, wearing an all-white T-shirt and cowboy boots to fit in with the locals. The boy who had wanted to be Captain America, to fight and die on the battlefield with honor, had been brought low not by war but by a bar fight behind a honky-tonk. That truth haunted me more than the scar ever would.

That was my rock bottom.

For weeks, I walked past that chain-link fence that separated the 25th Infantry Division from the 75th Ranger Regiment, and every time it was like a knife in the ribs. I could see them drilling, hear their cadence, even pick out faces I had trained and sweated beside. They were right there, my brothers, close enough that I could hear their voices echo across the motor pool, close enough to smell their PT shirts after morning runs. And yet I was no longer one of them. I was close enough to watch, but too far to belong. That fence might as well have been a wall a thousand feet high and a thousand miles wide. I used to catch myself gripping the cold steel wire, watching them move as a formation, my formation, until my knuckles turned white. Then I'd let go, slip back to my side of the fence, and carry that emptiness with me. That fence divided more than two units. It divided who I was from who I thought I would be. Every morning, that walk past the wire was a punishment, a reminder of what I had lost and could not get back.

In my head, my career was over. The Captain America dream was over. I thought I had thrown it all away in one night of rage and pride, that I had lost the only tribe I had ever wanted to be part of. I told myself I would never again stand among warriors of that caliber. The humiliation was worse than the pain. The ear healed, more or less, but the ache of losing the Regiment did not. In those weeks, I stopped seeing myself as a Ranger. I was just another soldier with a chewed-up ear and a broken dream.

What I couldn't see then was that my story wasn't over. The Army wasn't done with me. My life as a soldier and Ranger wasn't finished because of one alley fight. I would go on to serve in other great formations of Rangers, airborne infantry, and warriors. I would find new tribes. I would train and forge other Rangers. I would learn new lessons. I would even find myself in places and situations that would test me more than Pepper ever could.

But in those first weeks, standing on the wrong side of the wire with a bandaged ear and a broken dream, I believed it was all gone.

LESSON: RESPECT

Respect is one of the most misunderstood values among young men, young soldiers, and even many adults. At its core, respect is a positive feeling, admiration for someone's character, ability, or achievements. It is not the same as honor, though the two often get tangled together. Honor is about esteem, even prestige. Respect is deeper. It is not demanded, it is not taken, and it cannot be forced. Respect is earned.

In my youth, I believed the opposite. Like so many young warriors, I thought if someone disrespected me, or, worse, disrespected my tribe, then a fight was the only way forward. That mindset leads down dark avenues. You tell yourself that respect is something you have to defend at all costs and that the mere perception of disrespect justifies violence or revenge. That thinking destroys lives. It nearly destroyed mine.

Through time and service, I learned the truth. Respect is not something you shout about or fight for. It is something you build, patiently, through actions and excellence. True professionals, true leaders, the giants in any field, whether military, business, sports, or scholarship, do not demand respect. They earn it. And because it is earned, it lasts.

The danger is in making disrespect your measure of identity. I learned that the hard way in an alley behind a nightclub. I thought I was fighting for honor. I thought I was defending the Regiment. In reality, I was being driven by pride and immaturity. I ended up scarred, cut off from the tribe I loved, and walking a different path than the one I believed was my destiny. The scar on my ear is permanent, but the deeper wound was realizing how badly I misunderstood what respect really means.

That lesson is one I now try to pass on to my soldiers, my students, and especially my children. You do not have to fight to protect your respect. You do not have to demand it from others. You live your life in a way that earns it or you do not. And you respect others because it is right, not because of what they give you in return.

So when I see my kids argue over fairness or what someone said or did to them, I stop them. Respect is not a prize you seize in the moment. It is a life lived with integrity, consistency, and care for others. The only respect that matters is the kind you earn through your actions, your choices, and your excellence. My scar reminds me of that truth every day, a permanent mark of the folly of my youth and the price of confusing pride for respect.

If you want to know how to truly live strong, earn respect through how you show up, not through what you demand. Earn it in silence. Earn it in service. Earn it in the way others can trust your word and rely on your character. That kind of respect doesn't fade. It doesn't scar. It builds a legacy worth carrying.

DEFYING GRAVITY I

OF ALL THE REASONS NOT to pick a fight with Pepper, I had overlooked the one that would haunt me the most: My back was already injured. I just didn't know how bad it was yet.

I was having back trouble. Still have it, actually, thirty years later. For half my adult life, over fifteen years, I couldn't sleep in a bed. Too risky. Had to rack out on the floor or any available hard surface. Two years ago, I finally got one of those stiff foam memory mattress pads, and it's amazing. A whole new dream world. The funny thing is that when people see me today and ask about my ear, I can laugh and tell the story. When they ask about my back, the laughter isn't as quick. It is the ghost that has followed me the longest.

How did I mess myself up at twenty? It happened in a flash. Gravity was a factor. A force I respect and generally get along with, but on three occasions it nearly killed me. This was one of them.

The Army has a few basic ways it trains you to exit an aircraft. One is rappelling out of a helicopter. You wear a harness clipped to a rope with a carabiner, and those ropes are relatively thin, just strong enough to hold your weight but narrow enough that you can control your descent hand over hand. Even if you slip, you are still attached to it. Another is parachuting. You are strapped into a static line that automatically pulls your chute open the instant you step out of the plane. In both of those methods, the Army has engineered systems to keep you alive if you make a mistake.

Fast-roping is not like that. The rope itself is different: not thin, but thick, like a fireman's pole, and that is the basic idea. You don't clip in. You don't snap on a harness. You literally step into midair from the side of a helicopter, turn your body as you drop, and grab hold. Once you latch on, you slide down the rope the way a fireman drops from the second floor to the fire truck bay. Your gloved hands and the squeeze of your boots are the only things keeping you attached. Miss the rope, and you are free-falling. Get a bad grip, and you are still falling. There is no backup, no safety line, no parachute waiting to save you. This is why only special operations units are trained to fast-rope. It is one of the highest-risk insertion methods the Army has. But it does get soldiers to the ground quickly, sometimes too quickly.

That was the environment at Fort Lewis. Our Ranger battalion trained on both helicopters and a tall wooden tower built out in the woods.

We were on the tower one day. It rose somewhere between sixty and a hundred feet, tall enough to replicate a helicopter hover. The smell wasn't oil or cordite. It was pine from the surrounding forest, the acrid bite of burned rope, leather gloves singed from too much friction, and the sweat of hundreds of Rangers who had gone down before me. The tower was scarred and blackened from countless slides, the ropes thick with wear. There was always that nervous silence as each man stepped up to the edge, trying to look calm, while the truth was that everyone knew gravity was waiting.

I got a decent grasp and rotated off the ledge. At first it was going well. The vibration in my boots, the heat in my palms, the rope pressing through the gloves, the ground rushing up fast. Too fast. In that moment you know you are no longer in control—you are a passenger in gravity's grip. As the dirt rushed up toward me, I knew I was in trouble. Too late to slow myself. I spread my feet in the proper landing position, braced, and prayed.

The impact was like lightning exploding up my legs, a red-hot spike driving straight into my spine. I hit, toppled, and for a moment thought I might be paralyzed. It wasn't just the landing either. I was part of a mortar team, lugging extra weight: the base plate strapped to my rucksack, fifteen pounds of steel plus dummy rounds. That combination of weight, speed, and impact was the perfect storm. Pain flared like fire in my waist, but there is no crying in the Rangers. I forced myself up, narrowed my awareness to the next task, and somehow stumbled to where I was supposed to be.

I figured a weekend of rest would fix it. Friday night I racked out on the floor, popped Motrin, and stayed quiet. In the Army, Motrin is the cure-all. Back pain? Motrin. Sprain? Motrin. Bullet wound? The joke was always this: "Take 800 milligrams, drink water, and drive on." By Monday, though, the pain was worse. Weeks passed, and I was limping on runs, though oddly the limp faded the longer I ran. Finally, I bit the bullet and saw the doc.

He sucked his pen, studying the X-ray. "Lumbar compression fracture," he said flatly.

L4 and L5, smashed together, discs crushed, an indent in L5. He handed me the prescription every soldier knows too well: "Keep your core strong. Take 800 milligrams of Motrin for a few weeks. Come back later."

I was twenty. Mind-over-body unstoppable. "Pain is weakness leaving your body!" the guy yells in the movie *Platoon*. I took the pain. Slowly, I recovered enough that I no longer limped. Drove on with my career, never giving it another thought.

I jumped out of planes, ran miles, fought Pepper, fought in Iraq. Through it all, I had "good back" weeks, sometimes months, and then flare-ups so bad I could barely move. Sciatica down my legs, days when a wrong twist dropped me flat. But that was my life. You are dealt cards—you play them.

Over a decade passed. In that span, I lived the soldier's life at full throttle. I trained, deployed, competed in the Best Ranger Competition, and pushed my body through endless runs, ruck marches, obstacle courses, and parachute jumps. There were times the back felt almost normal, enough that I could pretend the injury had faded. Other times it roared back to remind me. The truth was it had never gone away. I just refused to admit it.

After a round of sciatica that would not go away, another Army doctor, this time at Fort Benning, looked at my X-rays and went pale. He took off his glasses, sat me down, and started talking like he was breaking the news of cancer. In fact, he told me he'd had conversations exactly like this with patients he had just diagnosed with cancer. He was that serious. "When did you break your back, Captain Spencer?"

"I've never broken my back," I said.

He shook his head slowly. "Your L5 vertebra is detached from your spine. Your back is broken right now."

"Well, medically speaking, maybe. I've certainly been high functioning all these years."

"Years?" he said, incredulous. We had a long talk. He did not believe it had been detached all that time. Likely weakened from the old injury and finally snapped after years of abuse. Training, jumps, the Best Ranger Competition, daily ten- to fifteen-mile runs, twenty-mile ruck marches. It had pushed me past the breaking point.

He offered surgery, of course. Pull the vertebra back, affix it with a metal frame. Success rate? "Thirty percent." Then he explained the 30 percent rule: 30 percent get better, 30 percent stay the same, 30 percent get worse. "And the other ten percent?" I asked. He did not answer. He looked at me the way a doctor looks when he knows you will not like any of the options.

My choice was the same as always. Surgery meant medical profile. Profile meant losing my assignment, maybe my career. I was thirty-two, and being a soldier was my identity. So I thanked him, collected the files, out-processed Fort Benning, and in-processed Fort Carson without mentioning a word. No lies, just omission. The Army was not asking a lot of questions. They needed bodies in Iraq.

What is my quality of life today? Well, from that point on it was sleeping on the floor. My idea of a "bad back" week changed. A wrong twist still drops me for weeks, the first few days walking like a ninety-year-old. Eventually it subsides. Keeping my core strong helps keep the good weeks going. Medicine has not advanced much—the 30 percent rule still holds. But 80 percent of the time I feel fine. Sleeping in a bed again is a win.

I sometimes joke that I am waiting for a sponsorship call.

"Hi, John Spencer here, for Ingalik. It is no fun being a warrior-scholar with a bad back. That is why I love my three-inch Gel Mattress Topper, ergonomically designed for today's rugged man of action. Call this number today, get fifteen percent off, and tell them the Ranger sent you!"

Maybe one day they will call. Until then, gravity and I remain in a complicated relationship.

LESSONS: SEE DEFYING GRAVITY III

CHAPTER 7

THE SOPRANOS OF BAGHDAD

ARRIVING AT AHMED'S FAVORITE CAFÉ, I nodded grimly to the young tough guy lingering just outside the door. He rapped three times. A gnarled fingertip parted the inside curtain, then the door was opened by Ahmed's "uncle," a grizzled consigliere who didn't bother hiding the burn scars across his bald head. He beckoned me and my guys to enter but halted us just inside.

The café itself was part neighborhood hangout, part throne room. Once, no doubt, it had been a respectable corner establishment. The walls were lined with cheap framed prints and one or two faded photographs of Iraqi leaders from another era, their glass panes clouded with age. The tile floor was cracked, and mismatched chairs had been shuffled around enough to leave scratches across the surface. Now, with its doors shuttered during midday, the room had been converted into a stage for Ahmed's power. The curtains kept out the harsh Baghdad sun, leaving the interior dim, except for the feeble glow of a single overhead bulb and the weak, colored light of a neon tea sign in the corner. The air was heavy—stale tobacco, burnt sugar from countless pots of chai, the faint scent of dust and sweat. And over it all, the wailing of an Arabic dirge seeping from a battered floor speaker.

Ahmed sat at his favorite table directly beneath an oil painting of the former king of Iraq, as though the monarch himself were lending legitimacy to his meetings. Fortyish and heavyset, dressed in a purple Adidas track suit that gleamed like armor in the dim room, he sipped his tea slowly, projecting calm and control. A man hunched forward across from him, speaking quickly, nervously. Ahmed listened impassively, his dark eyes fixed, his features unmoving, except for the occasional small nod. The stillness was itself a performance.

Aside from Uncle, the only other people were two men seated at a side table. They weren't customers. The café wasn't open to the public during these hours, which made it plain this was business. Both men sat with AK-47s resting casually across their laps, their fingers idly drumming on the wooden stocks. Their eyes were on us from the moment we entered, unblinking, assessing.

It was unusual for Ahmed to admit us when he had another visitor, and I looked at Brad inquiringly. His name wasn't really Brad, nor was he American. He was my interpreter, an Iraqi architecture student whose American nickname had stuck. Brad raised an eyebrow at me as if to say: *Wait it out, sir.* He was calm. He had been doing this for six years, translating for one rotation of American units after another. He knew how Ahmed worked.

But Staff Sergeant Fitz, my convoy leader and bodyguard, didn't look reassured. He was charged with my safety, and he saw what I saw: two armed men at the table, Uncle within arm's reach of whatever he had beneath his vest, and the room's atmosphere tense enough to ignite. Fitz shifted slightly by the door, rifle slung but ready, eyes sharp, reading every angle and distance. He was steady, but I could tell by his clenched jaw he was ready for the worst.

Ahmed's visitor looked back at us nervously, but Ahmed waved him on. And then I understood: Ahmed wanted the man to see me, a US officer, standing there waiting. It was theater. Ahmed didn't just conduct business; he staged it. Everything, the posture, the tea, the dirge, the painting of the king, was performance.

The man finished his plea. Ahmed took a long pause, staring off into the middle distance as though weighing matters of state, then spoke a few quiet words. The man sagged in disappointment, nodded, and withdrew. Ahmed dismissed him with a flick of his wrist. Uncle ushered him out.

The moment the curtain fell back, Ahmed's face transformed. Stern ruler turned genial host. He rose slightly, smiling. "Captain Spencer, my dear friend! Sorry to keep you waiting. So many things I must attend to!"

Brad and I stepped closer. Fitz stayed at the door where I'd placed him, a buffer between us and the AKs. I sat across from Ahmed while Brad took the chair beside me.

"How is your blessed mother in her great illness, Captain?" Ahmed asked.

This was one of his rituals. In our first meeting he had told me of his own mother's sickness, and I had mentioned mine. Ever since, he began every session with this exchange, as if we were not officer and gangster but two sons bound by duty to our mothers. It was part of the game. I thanked him, and he assured me Allah was merciful.

Then came the sigh. Ahmed leaned back, letting it roll across the table like smoke. "Captain, I am much saddened by the unwise decision of your superiors last week."

It was a softer opening than I had expected. The issue was money. American money that once passed through Ahmed's hands was now being paid directly to the guards he employed. My job was to ease that sting.

Brad translated my reply carefully. "It is better those guards are paid directly by us, Ahmed. The Army no longer wishes to deal with middlemen."

"I am not the middle, my friend," Ahmed countered smoothly. "I am the holy man perched atop the mountain."

"Be that as it may, we prefer to do things our way."

Ahmed sipped his tea, then shook his head slowly, sadly. "The men earn less this way, you know. And the longer it continues, the more they will resent you."

"They earn more, Ahmed. They keep one hundred percent of what we promised them."

"Ah. You say that because I no longer collect a fee. But our men uphold this practice regardless of who pays. As soon as you gave them the money, they ran to me. To beg my forgiveness, to pay tribute. But here is the truth, Captain: They gave me more than I ever withheld. Why? Because I am generous. So, you see, if the dollars come directly from you, they will always have less."

It was dizzying logic, a world turned upside down. "I don't buy it."

Ahmed spread his hands. "Is it hard to believe? You see my men every day, Captain. Ask them. Ask anyone."

I glanced at Brad. His eyes told me Ahmed wasn't bluffing. Our bean counters thought they could sidestep him. They didn't understand how tribute worked, how loyalty was enforced. Ahmed's power wasn't only in what he took. It was in the way men *chose* to give more than he demanded because to be in his favor meant safety. To be outside it meant trouble.

And that was the truth of Baghdad. We were trying to build democracy through envelopes of hundred-dollar bills delivered to gangsters in track suits.

The Coalition forces deployed in 2003, to include me, had been chosen to defeat the Iraqi military. We accomplished that mission in twenty days. What followed was far more complicated. For the next eight years we were tasked with policing an entire country, rebuilding Iraq's shattered infrastructure, and supporting a complete overhaul of its economy and political process, much as General MacArthur had done in postwar Japan. What the media regularly portrayed as an endless hostile foreign occupation was in reality tens of thousands of soldiers and civilians working themselves ragged each day to serve a traumatized population. It was less the image of conquerors and more the reality of exhausted men and women trying to keep the lights on, the water flowing, and the streets safe in an impoverished nation still staggering under decades of dictatorship.

Frustrating our efforts was an array of insurgent factions who did not want Iraq to be shepherded by infidels or "corrupted" by our modern, Western, secular ideals. These terrorists attacked foreign-aid projects and Coalition troops and worked tirelessly to force their warped ideas on local communities. Every terrorist chief fancied himself the next ruler of the nation, just as Saddam Hussein had schemed and murdered his way to the top thirty years before.

To properly secure a nation of twenty-four million, civil and defense experts estimated the Coalition needed a million personnel on the ground. We had less than a fifth of that. Even as we trained new Iraqi military and police forces, we lacked the manpower to protect every rural province and urban neighborhood. In a region called Al-Anbar, terrorists had moved so aggressively against local tribes that the offended leaders decided they'd rather cooperate with the American military. They agreed their own men would patrol the neighborhoods, as well as provide us with information about the bad guys. This initiative was called the "Sunni Awakening," and the idea was to expand it all across the country, in both rural and urban areas. Both the American and Iraqi governments would reimburse the tribes for these security operations. Across the country then, armed bands like our local Sons of Iraq were created. In the urban areas, it was much less about tribes but rather gangs managed by Tony Soprano types like Ahmed. Shady operators with fingers in every local pie, they knew every man in their neighborhoods and that man's extended family. Ahmed chose all the tough guys who manned the checkpoints in and out of his territory. Did that make him a hero of the new democracy? No. He was a street boss, a black marketeer, and probably a killer. But we couldn't have run the place without him.

Our payroll discussion was over. I agreed I would recommend to my battalion commander that we go back to providing a weekly satchel of crisp $100 bills for Ahmed to distribute as he saw fit, often in payday activities organized to put Coalition forces at ease while keeping power where it had to be. The arrangement gave everyone the illusion of order, but in truth it reinforced Ahmed's role as the gatekeeper. Money flowed, men lined up, the guards got their wages, and we could tell ourselves the system was working. Ahmed smiled because everyone in the room knew the power still flowed through him. I moved on to other business. Teenage hustlers were always hanging around the US bases trying to sell bootleg DVDs. Ahmed agreed it was terrible, but what could he do?

I sensed something going on behind me. Glancing back, I saw Uncle was speaking to someone outside through a crack in the door. He turned, asked Ahmed something, and the boss responded tersely. Before Brad could translate, Uncle was opening the door for two new guys.

I knew the first. Najib was a lanky man about my age with bushy hair and a sharp, restless gaze. He was another Ahmed, the boss of the neighborhood half a klick west of us. Unlike Ahmed, he made no attempt to play the magnanimous Godfather. His whole bearing was harder, leaner, more like a street pimp who would slit your throat for looking at him wrong. The goon behind him, clearly one of the pimp's muscle, carried himself like a man itching for a fight. A fat pistol grip stuck brazenly out of his waistband, meant to be seen as much as used. The temperature in the room seemed to rise. Ahmed's riflemen tensed, their hands settling more firmly on their weapons. Uncle's eyes narrowed to slits, his scarred head angling toward the intruders. Staff Sergeant Fitz read the tension instantly and slid a half step closer to Ahmed's men, adjusting his stance to give the newcomers just enough breathing room without ceding any ground.

Ahmed was all smiles. "My dear friend Najib, what a delightful surprise! May I conclude my business with Captain Spencer? And then I shall be entirely yours."

Najib stared icily at him. Pretending not to notice, Ahmed turned the music down a notch, then addressed me. "I have thought about your Civil Affairs' plan to start delivering large dumpsters in the neighborhood so everyone stops throwing it in the streets."

I knew what he was doing. Making Najib wait. Letting Najib overhear us. As if Ahmed was the kingpin, and I, the hapless US Army officer, had come hat in hand to seek his counsel.

Ahmed started naming local drivers who might agree to the work. Najib listened, seething, until his patience finally broke. "Ahmed! What about my sister's boy?"

Brad was at my ear, rapidly translating:

"Quite unfortunate," Ahmed admitted. "But that is how headstrong young men behave."

"They shot him! Like a mangy dog in the street! And now they walk around, smiling?"

Now I knew the beef: One of Najib's guys had refused to stop for an Ahmed checkpoint.

Ahmed shrugged. "Had it occurred in your territory, your men would've done the same."

Najib's eyeballs bugged out. He started to sputter, but Ahmed calmly raised a palm. "You are being discourteous. I am speaking to Captain Spencer."

"Captain Spencer can go to the devil!"

His fists were balled in rage, and the look in his eyes was the one my mom used to get just before she erupted. Only the weapons here were a lot worse than a belt.

Najib's man's hand went closer to his gun.

Uncle, likewise, reached toward his vest, the table guards leveled their AKs, and Fitz's eyes went wide. In a flash, all three of us saw how precarious our position was. If anyone in that room said or did the wrong thing in the next few seconds, we'd all be lying in a pool of blood.

I was an Airborne Ranger. Trained to destroy enemy troops. How had I wound up here?

Having finished my first combat tour in Iraq four years before, I was grateful to draw an assignment that allowed me some time to reflect on where I'd been and what I might do next.

Ironically, it was in a place most soldiers do not find relaxing or contemplative: Ranger School.

Years ago, I'd been a candidate there. Then I became an instructor, one of those mysterious figures on the class periphery who sees everything and offers occasional wisdom, but you never know what they're really thinking. Mostly, I was thinking how nice it was not to have death close at hand. There's plenty of pain at Ranger School, of course. Candidates regularly suffer injury, exhaustion, and humiliation, but nobody dies. We instructors made sure of that, just as the instructors in my day made sure we didn't die.

Being an instructor also provided important opportunities for my professional development. Planning and the written dissemination of command intent had been one of my strengths as a platoon leader, but now I had the time to truly master the craft of formulating, processing, and expressing myself. At thirty years old, I was a seasoned leader in the field, but moving forward meant acquiring the skills required for higher command and for the responsibilities of a staff officer. Ranger School forced me to refine those habits. I had to think more clearly, write more concisely, and communicate in a way that others could act on without hesitation. At the same time, I discovered that I genuinely enjoyed teaching. Watching young soldiers, and later cadets, grasp a concept or apply a lesson was rewarding in a way that was different from leading soldiers in combat—yet complementary to it. One was about shaping lives and developing minds, the other about guiding men through the chaos of battle. Together they revealed the full spectrum of what it meant to be a leader.

I also knew I might end up back in Iraq, though any return would be at least a year away. I'd finish my stint as a Ranger instructor, then get assigned to a new unit, which could be sent to the Middle East or Afghanistan at some point. There was no way to predict who they needed.

What I hadn't counted on was a personal invitation.

"Captain Spencer, there's a company command opening in Baghdad. They need a combat veteran with war fighting skills and max enthusiasm—do you want combat command?"

There is no answer for an Airborne Ranger officer to that question other than, "*Yes sir!*" I didn't need to hear another word. Such opportunities only came once in a blue moon and were pretty much a golden ticket to whatever you wanted to do for the rest of your career. The next bit threw me for a bit of a loop, though.

"It's the 68th Armor Regiment. You'll have a mix of tanks and mech infantry."

Mech infantry soldiers deploy in Bradley fighting vehicles, and their officers train extensively with those vehicles. I'd never even ridden in one. Or a tank.

I told them that. They didn't care.

"Truth is, Captain, we've got a mess on our hands. Just get in there. You can figure it out as you go."

Heavy equipment was the least of my problems. Every Army outpost in Baghdad was now another Fort Apache, with more terrorists just outside the T-walls than ever. They needed warriors, but the brass had decided we needed to ramp up "civic engagement" as well. So I wasn't just the company commander but also mayor and sheriff of three wildly overcrowded city neighborhoods of Baghdad. Everything that went on in my sector was my responsibility. And everything that went wrong was my fault. I needed eyes and ears on every block. Then I became the payroll master because Iraqi Ministry of Interior officials couldn't drive around with stacks of cash.

That's how I wound up on a first-name basis with the Sopranos of Baghdad.

In the tearoom, Ahmed stared icily, daring the rival boss to make some dumb move. I knew both chieftains were crafty, but their goons were wild cards. Hotheads, punks on the make.

I slowly raised my palms, speaking soothingly, and Brad matched my tone: "Gentlemen. We are all friends here."

That wasn't true. Shooting Najib's nephew was like dumping gasoline on a roaring blaze. All I could hope was that neither boss wanted to die over such petty grief. Not that either would give an inch in the moment, of course. It was the same story all over Iraq, actually: bad guys, worse guys, and US troops caught in the middle.

"The young man seems to have made a huge mistake in his actions," I told Ahmed. "But the bullet struck his face, and he is disfigured."

"They told him to stop. He disobeyed."

I looked to Najib. "I know Ahmed, and he is a generous man. Is there some compensation your family might accept?" I had been in Iraq long enough to know a tribal or even cultural settlement for wrongful deaths could be paid in what we called "blood money."

Najib sneered. "The only thing I will accept is his head on a stick!"

Seemingly bored with all this posturing, Ahmed waved casually. "Half a million dinar."

Najib exploded in outrage. "*Half a million?* Four million!"

"The boy is injured, but he lives."

"Three million, you cringing jackal, or I'll kill you where you stand!"

"I'm not standing, Najib. One million. Or you will be dead before you hit the floor."

Najib cast his eyes slowly about the room. Uncle stood like iron, ready to die. The two guards at the table and Sergeant Fitz were remarkably steely. Any shooting, he'd be the first to fall. Najib's eyes locked on mine like lasers. I didn't appear to be armed but in fact had my 9 mm pistol ready under the table.

All things considered, a million dinar was nothing to sneeze at, so Najib finally nodded. "Allah is good."

I slowly exhaled.

"I don't have it here," Ahmed cautioned.

"You are a man of your word," Najib allowed. "Just take care this never happens again."

He nodded to his man, and Uncle let them out, death staring them every step of the way.

Brad was quavering beside me, as Sergeant Fitz slowly rolled the tension out of his neck.

And Ahmed? Just another day at the office. He smiled benevolently as we stood. "It was a pleasure to see you as always, my captain. Please extend my fondest wishes to your mother."

LESSON: HUMILITY

The Sopranos of Baghdad chapter may read like a gangster movie set in the middle of a war zone, but for me it was one of the hardest and most important lessons I carried forward. The lesson is simple to say but difficult to live: *Be humble.*

In the military, in business, and in life, people often tell you to be aggressive, to be the smartest in the room, the toughest, the most lethal. I have lived that world, and yes, there is a place for strength and resolve. But there is also greatness in humility. The real honor is not the honor we receive; it is the honor we give.

General James Mattis, famously called Mad Dog and Chaos, once advised Marines to be polite and professional but to have a plan to kill everybody they meet. It is a sharp reminder of what combat demands. But what is often overlooked is the power of humility, even in those moments. Humility does not mean weakness. It means listening. It means accepting you do not know everything. It means remembering that even in a position of authority, you still have something to learn.

That day in Baghdad, I had rank and a pistol, but I was a guest in Ahmed's café. The rules of that block, of that city, were not mine.

They belonged to men who enforced their own codes of honor, disrespect, and blood money. To survive, I had to be humble. Humble enough to listen, to acknowledge limits, and to navigate a culture I did not fully understand. That humility did not make me less of a soldier. It kept me and my men alive.

When I took command of a mechanized infantry unit, even though my background was as an Airborne Ranger, I definitely had to be humble. I could not pretend to be the technical expert on every vehicle or weapon system, but I could be the tactical expert who listened, learned, and gave others respect. Humility was the bridge that kept the organization together.

Being humble is not about lowering yourself. It is about raising others, giving them respect whether they have earned it yet or not. It is about knowing you are part of something bigger than yourself. You do not have to be the loudest, the toughest, or the smartest in the room. In fact, if you are, you are probably failing to develop the people around you.

Humility is not a weaker position. It is an attribute that has saved my life more than once, including that day in Baghdad surrounded by gangsters, rifles, and blood feuds. The real strength is not pride; it is humility.

CHAPTER 8

TEST FIRE

YEAH, I GOT TO BE *that* hero. For a few weeks, anyway.

I am talking about the full Army of Liberation Welcome Wagon rollout. Iraqi crowds surged into the streets as our war chariots crawled forward, the crush of bodies so thick the Humvees could barely crawl an inch at a time. Dust and sweat rolled off the people pressing against our doors. Faces leaned into our windows, mouths open in chants we could not understand, the roar vibrating in our chests. Hands clawed for our sleeves and helmets as if one touch would guarantee the future they suddenly believed in. The smell of sweat, exhaust, and burning trash hung over everything. Flower petals floated down and stuck to the grime on our uniforms and windshields. It was a scene out of a Paris newsreel after World War II, only here it felt suffocating, as if the crowd might swallow us whole. Parents hoisted little girls in bright dresses, some in gowns as if for a wedding procession, holding them high above the press of bodies with smiles that seemed to say, *Our children are safe now. Our future is safe.*

Inside the vehicles, we forced ourselves to sit steady, rifles slung but within easy reach. The drivers inched forward, nudging the horns, although the sound vanished in the tidal roar around us. The flood of voices, the pressed-in faces, the laughter and cries of joy were overwhelming, and part of us wanted to be carried along by it. Yet every soldier in my platoon knew how fast a crowd could turn. One spark, a gunshot, a rumor, even a shove in the wrong place, and our convoy could be devoured whole. Behind the bullet-proof glass my men looked calm, but their eyes darted, their hands brushed triggers, and the truth was plain in the way their shoulders stayed tight. Celebration and danger pressed against us in the same breath.

That was my column of eight Humvees back in 2003, rolling at a crawl into the northern Iraqi city of Irbil, then on toward Kirkuk. This was Kurdish country. These people had suffered under Saddam's heel for decades. They had been gassed in the north, hunted in their villages, imprisoned without trial, and disappeared by the tens of thousands. Every family had a story, and many carried scars that could not be hidden. So when they saw American forces driving openly through their streets, they did not need a television broadcast to explain what it meant. They knew we had fought the Iraqi Army. They knew what our vehicles and uniforms symbolized: the end of the dictator who had tormented them. Their celebration was not symbolic or distant. It was personal, rooted in memory, and written in blood.

I tried to keep it in perspective. My platoon's six weeks on the ground had been anything but easy. We had already fought our share of engagements, but the cheers of the Kurds pressed in louder than the doubts, louder than the dust, louder than the fatigue. I had not joined the Army out of some idealistic dream of helping people. I joined because I wanted to be a soldier, to test myself in the hardest profession, and to measure up against its standards. Yet here in this corner of Iraq, the two aims overlapped. The oppressed were free enough to flood into the streets, to wave and cheer, to press food and flowers toward us, to offer whatever they had. For that brief moment, all the weight of years of service seemed to balance. It felt justified.

There was a sense that maybe the hardest part was behind us. Kirkuk, with its jubilation and flower petals, might actually be a good place to spend the next fifty days. That was the unofficial word making its way through the ranks. It came straight from the two-star general who boarded our plane before we left Italy and declared with certainty that our conquest of Iraq would last *at most* ninety days. His confidence was contagious. We believed him because we wanted to believe him.

The enemy was defeated, or so it appeared. Our orders were to mop up, to dismantle what was left of Saddam's machine, to gather up weapons, and to clear the way for whatever government came next. It sounded like basic grunt work, tedious but manageable. Compared to dodging bullets, RPGs, or Silkworm missiles, it felt almost like a reprieve.

It took less than a day to realize that cleanup was not going to be the break we had imagined. The word itself suggested sweeping up debris, securing a few empty bunkers, maybe pulling a little guard duty before heading home. Instead, the reality came crashing down almost immediately. The tasks multiplied, the demands grew heavier, and the illusion of an easy end to the war dissolved before we had even settled in.

One: We had more to do than any platoon could reasonably handle. Manhunts for the fifty-two most-wanted Ba'ath Party fugitives were priority, but they were only the start. We were also expected to guard power stations, fuel depots, and government buildings. Every day meant collecting the weapons and vehicles abandoned by Saddam's collapsing forces, never knowing if the next pile would be a few rifles or a warehouse stacked floor to ceiling. On top of that hung the search for the hidden weapons of mass destruction that everyone believed were still out there, waiting to be found.

Two: The Iraqis expected us to deal with every problem that surfaced. Criminal complaints came to our checkpoints. Farmers asked us about irrigation and broken pumps. People demanded answers about sanitation, power outages, and the failing grid. We were soldiers, yet we were suddenly responsible for the work of mayors, judges, and city engineers. Under Saddam it had all been handled by force, but at least there was an iron system. Take him away and Iraq was...nothing. A blank space. A country without a plan, and now it was on us to fill it.

That was the blank that nobody had worried about before we went in. The assumption was that Iraqi exiles who had lived in the West would return, slip into office, and guide the country forward. Others believed the Iraqi people themselves, once freed from tyranny, would simply know what to do. None of it happened. Six weeks after our boots hit the ground, there was no new government, no smooth transition, only a nation hollowed out by decades of dictatorship. Saddam and his cronies had drained the country of competence as well as hope. Japan and Germany had not rebuilt themselves in weeks, months, or even years, and Iraq was no different. After World War II, American soldiers stayed in those nations for decades. Now the mission handed to us was the same, though dressed up with a new term: "SASO"—Security and Stability Operations. And it was suddenly on our plate too.

Our first real brush with the locals came when my platoon escorted a tanker truck of water into a parched Kirkuk neighborhood. Even before our convoy reached the square, people poured into the street, shouting, waving buckets and plastic jugs, pressing toward the truck like it was salvation. By the time we pulled over, it was a full-blown mob. Housewives elbowed their way forward, kids darted between legs, old men shouted, and the whole square turned into a desperate block party. We could not understand a word, only the tone—urgent, demanding, pleading all at once. I had my men try to form a line, talking loud enough to be heard without sounding like we were barking orders. "Keep weapons slung," I told them. Look calm. Do not look like an occupying army passing out charity. For all my Ranger training, I suddenly found myself trying to direct traffic, herd children, and manage a water line in a language I did not speak.

I was standing beside my Humvee, trying to wave people into some kind of order, when the first blast hit. *Boom!*—a detonation so loud it seemed to lift the ground under our boots. A column of flame rose just a few blocks west, the fireball rolling over the rooftops like something out of a nightmare. For a split second I thought we were under attack, that Saddam loyalists had opened up on us with artillery or rockets. The crowd thought the same. Screams cut through the smoke as hundreds of people broke and ran in every direction, containers and buckets clattering to the ground. I spun, looking for my men through the haze, shouting over the roar, "What the hell was that?"

Then a second explosion tore through the air, closer this time, the concussion rattling our vehicles and echoing down the narrow streets. A third followed almost immediately, the blasts rolling toward us in a pattern that could only mean a chain reaction. Each detonation seemed to leapfrog the last, fire and smoke rising in stages, the sound pounding through our chests. My men ducked behind doors and corners, eyes wide, not sure if we were caught in a deliberate attack or watching half the neighborhood go up in flames on its own.

Thick, oily plumes coiled upward, blotting the sky like a black curtain. The fire roared and shifted with a life of its own, brilliant orange flashes bursting inside the smoke as if the whole block had become a furnace. For a moment it felt unreal, almost like watching a staged demolition or a fireworks display. Then the truth sank in. This was no attack. Some hidden stockpile of weapons or ammunition had ignited, each explosion setting off the next, the fire leaping from one structure to another, as if the whole neighborhood were primed to blow.

Then came a fourth explosion, even stronger than the last, and a fifth that felt like it was aimed directly at us. A wall of fire and smoke surged forward, a towering wave that seemed ready to consume everything in its path. The heat rolled over us so intensely it felt like opening an oven door the size of a city block. The air was sharp with chemicals and burning fuel. Bits of debris and charred paper scraps spun down in the wind and stuck to our gear like black snow.

Sergeant First Class Herring came running through the haze, his face lit orange by the flames behind him. "Sir, we need to get out of here now!" His voice carried the edge of urgency that left no room for debate. Around us my soldiers were already shifting uneasily, glancing from the rolling fireball to me, waiting for the call. The awe of the moment was gone. It was time to move.

I did not argue. I started shouting orders, my voice straining to rise above the roar of the fire and the clatter of the crowd still fleeing down the streets. My men scrambled back to their positions, slamming into Humvees, waving the water truck forward. Engines revved, gears ground, and one by one the vehicles lurched into motion. We pushed hard to get clear, the tanker swaying on its axles as it rumbled out of the square, my own Humvee right behind it. The fire kept booming behind us, each blast a reminder that we were seconds away from being engulfed if we stayed.

Not every day came with fireballs and chaos. Most days were slower, quieter, and in many ways harder. We were far from the center of action. The Big Picture was unfolding in Baghdad, where the Coalition Provisional Authority was walling itself into one of Saddam's palaces and calling it the Green Zone. Our world was the north—Kirkuk, the surrounding towns and villages, and thousands of square miles of empty hills and plains. It felt remote, like we were holding the edges of a map while the real story was being written elsewhere.

My memories are mostly of driving down long, lonely roads across rugged, barren land. Keeping our eyes open. Checking this place or that, setting up checkpoints, or checking on checkpoints. For the first forty-eight hours after Kirkuk fell, Kurdish fighters who had fought alongside us against Saddam's forces had free rein. We watched them stream north with whatever they could seize. Some rode captured tanks, engines belching black smoke, men clinging to the hulls and turrets, waving rifles in celebration. It did not take long before the order came down to stop that. From then on, every vehicle had to be inspected. Cars, trucks, tractors, dump trucks piled high with goods. We were looking for Ba'ath Party fugitives, contraband, and weapons and also keeping track of what was leaving the city before the whole country was stripped bare.

Most of it was routine, but sometimes it was not. Another platoon from our battalion stopped a dump truck that looked unremarkable at first glance. Three nervous men sat in the cab, insisting they were hauling copper. When the tarp came back, the bars underneath did not shine like anything from Fort Knox. They were dull, almost copper in color, the kind of crude, unfinished ingots that could easily fool a tired checkpoint team into waving them on.

For a moment the story seemed believable. But something about it did not sound or feel right to the soldier on scene. He trusted his gut and called it in for a closer look. That instinct proved correct. What they had in the truck was not copper at all but 999 bars of gold.

The discovery made headlines around the world. CNN ran it under the title, "US Troops Find $250 Million in Gold Hidden in Truck" (May 27, 2003).

The truck was brought back and parked inside the wire at our brigade headquarters. For a short time, it sat there like something out of a pirate story, treasure stacked and waiting. Temptation proved too much for one soldier. That night he snuck into the truck, slipped a bar into his rucksack, and thought he had gotten away with it. He was caught, and from then on guards had to be posted around the clock until the gold was picked up and taken away to some unknown vault.

Not long after, I had my own brush with temptation at one of our checkpoints. We were stopping every vehicle that came through, searching for weapons or anything suspicious. Most of the time it was beat-up sedans, dusty trucks, or tractors pulling carts. Then one day a spotless new Mercedes Benz rolled up, gleaming like it had just come off the showroom floor. That alone was enough to raise eyebrows.

When we searched the vehicle, we found a briefcase on the back seat. Inside was a stack of crisp US hundred-dollar bills totaling twenty thousand dollars. Brigade policy required us to report any amount over ten thousand. The driver calmly explained that the money was his, that carrying it was not illegal, and that he had every right to do so. Technically, he was correct. We could not arrest him or seize the cash, but under the rules we were required to escort both him and the money to battalion headquarters for questioning.

That was not his preference. He opened the case again, peeled off ten thousand dollars, and offered it to me. Just like that. "Take it," he said. No questions. No escort. It would be mine if I wanted it. His tone was matter of fact, as if this were the most natural solution in the world.

I stood there with my radio telephone operator (RTO)—the soldier assigned to carry and monitor our military radio and hand me the handset when I needed it or if someone was calling me—at my shoulder, the only one close enough to see and hear what was happening. He did not say a word, but I knew he was watching. Soldiers notice everything. If I wavered even for a second, he would carry that knowledge with him.

I told the man no. He would be escorted to battalion with the money, exactly as the rules required. My RTO and I watched the Mercedes roll away under guard, and just like that the moment passed.

After that, it was back to the routine of soldiering. Any time we stopped near a settlement, people gathered. Some glad to see us, others scowling or needy, but we weren't equipped to win hearts and minds. Except some of the kids, with their curious little faces, gaping at us like we were Martians. Occasionally, one of us would dig into his MRE, find a stick of gum, or a pack of Skittles, and gift it to some wide-eyed urchin. The kids would try it, warily. Then the sugar hit their tongues, and they broke out in huge grins. That aside, we mostly pantomime directed the locals, politely and firmly, to keep their distance.

One day, a man who spoke English approached us and really wanted to thank us. He was a cab driver who ran afoul of Saddam's men and wound up getting tortured in prison. His English was so good I asked if he wanted a job, and I hired him on the spot as our first interpreter.

What kept us most occupied was all the tallying, transporting, and/or destroying every abandoned stockpile of weapons, equipment, vehicles, or ammo we could find. Even in the boondocks, Iraq was armed to the teeth. You'd think Saddam's forces would have been depleted by eight years fighting Iran in the 1980s, then his 1991 rout in Kuwait, but by 2003 his army was again one of the biggest in the world. And when it fell apart, plenty was left behind.

Our first major cleanup was K1 and K2, the two airports in Kirkuk. Both were seized early in the war and put to heavy use by Coalition supply flights. We were tasked to survey every dilapidated hangar and outbuilding scattered about the acres. Most were empty, but one day we crowbarred open a hangar door and discovered a veritable Home Depot of weapons and ammo. It took us days to catalog every box, carry it out, and truck it to our own secure bunkers. In some ways, it made sense that Saddam kept major depots up north because he feared uprisings by the hostile Kurdish minority. What we weren't prepared for was how many smaller caches we simply happened upon. Locals might tip us off about a suspicious shed or recent excavation, and sometimes we simply spotted unguarded stockpiles while driving around.

"Hey, what's that sticking out of the corn field?"

"Ooh, a surface-to-air missile launcher!"

Sometimes what we found struck me as too useless to move, so we draped everything in C4 explosive packs, stood back, and enjoyed the fireworks.

Did it occur to us we were actually in a race to find all this stuff?

Not at first. The Iraqi Army was no more, and people were adjusting to a life of freedom. There was certainly criminal activity in and around Kirkuk—organized smuggling and looting—but guys like that weren't beating the bushes for mobile artillery units or landmines.

Then the bombings started.

Homemade contraptions. The dreaded IEDs. Then people started getting shot—Iraqis, I mean, not us—in what were apparently revenge killings. Family feuds and personal grudges that went back decades. Saddam had also forcibly displaced thousands of Shi'ite families in Kirkuk, and now they were returning to reclaim their homes, by vicious force if necessary.

It got worse when people started shooting at *us*. We weren't party to any family feud; it was simply terrorism, anti-imperialist gestures by local gangsters or warlords eager to seize power. Bad guys who didn't want US troops playing sheriff or spreading the hated gospels of democracy, liberalism, Christianity, or internationalism.

That was the start of Phase 4, what the US military calls "stabilization" operations. Which went on for another eight years, cost us billions, and claimed untold lives. And what laid the groundwork for the insurgency were all those unsecured stockpiles. A cornucopia of lethality just waiting to be picked up by anyone passing by and used against us. I wish there were some specific event I could cite as the perfect metaphor for that brief idyll before all hell broke loose. Some grand, symbolic foreshadowing of all that was to come.

Actually, I *do* have one. Sometimes life provides exactly what art demands.

The town was Hawija, soon to be one of the deadliest terrorist battlegrounds in all Iraq. We were again conducting wide-ranging search operations—this time looking for rockets the growing insurgency was using on rails to launch at American positions. My platoon was sent to check out an airfield. No cache was found, but we did spot a tank ditch—basically a half-excavated rise of ground—against which someone had stacked about ten industrial-grade black barrels.

I don't know who suggested using this opportunity for a weapons check, but it was not unusual. Soldiers in combat are trained to keep their weapons clean, lubricated, and serviced almost religiously, but from time to time they also need to test-fire them to be certain they are ready to spring into action. That junk pile of barrels did not look like anything that required further investigation, so I requested radio permission from my company commander, and he granted us the OK to light it up, a simple test-fire of weapons.

My guys grinned. Nothing like some live fire to clear the senses! I gave the honor to the Mk 19 grenade launcher mounted atop my vehicle. It's basically a belt-fed 40 mm grenade machine gun that makes a distinctive *whomp, whomp, whomp* when fired, followed by a *boom, boom, boom*—methodical and beautiful in its symphony of destruction. We backed my Humvee up about three hundred meters. I didn't want to be any closer on the off chance those barrels were full of gasoline. The rest of the platoon waited another hundred meters behind us.

Brooks was above me in the vehicle gun hatch, sliding the large lever back to arm the Mk 19. When he looked to me for approval, I calmly announced, "Fire at will." Having blown up all kinds of stuff over the last month or so, I figured I had seen it all.

What I had never seen, before or since, was Time Stand Still.

The tank ditch vanished in an explosion I can only liken to slo-mo footage of moon shots blasting off from Cape Canaveral. Only this wasn't slo-mo, and we saw this immense white wall of the shockwave flying out to meet us. I just had time to duck behind my open driver's door before it hit us with a sound and fury unlike any I'd ever known. Nonlethal, thankfully, but a thing you actually felt pressing down into your guts.

When I was sure it was past and gone, I slowly rose and just stared, stunned.

A butte-sized column of smoke and fire was pouring into the sky, mushrooming out, and it just kept climbing. A mile high, maybe two. Maybe more. My stunned guys looked to each other, and to me. All of our ears were ringing, jaws unclenching, realizing we were lucky to be alive.

Radio static cut the wonder. It was my commanding officer. *"White 6, this is Attack 6! Was that you?"*

I swallowed, feeling so mortal and unworthy before the looming Hammer of the Gods. Raising the mic, I replied as blandly but confidently as I could, "Attack 6, this is White 6. Test fire complete."

There was no way to hide it anyway. The cloud streamed into the sky like a signal flare, visible for miles in every direction. Calls were already pouring in from units across the region, every one of them demanding to know what in God's name had just happened. It was not the kind of thing you could cover up. The sky itself told the story.

What those barrels most likely contained was solid propellant—rocket fuel. Literally the stuff that puts mega-missiles into space. And boy, did people notice. My captain was fielding concerned calls from units a hundred miles away. "*What the hell was that?*"

An omen, to be sure. That the victory parade was over.

Temptation came in many forms. Sometimes it was treasure stacked in a truck under guard. Sometimes it was a stranger on the roadside holding out a briefcase. And sometimes it was the urge to squeeze the trigger on a pile of barrels that looked harmless…until they almost took us with them. The test was always the same.

LESSON: INTEGRITY

From the day soldiers enter service, crossing the line from civilian to soldier, they are indoctrinated with a list of values. At first, they are memorized like multiplication tables. Over time, they are tested, sharpened, and proven in training and in combat until they are no longer words but character.

Integrity sits at the center of that list.

Any profession, any human relationship, is built on trust. Trust between a soldier and a commander, between a worker and a boss, between a husband and a wife, between a citizen and society. Once trust is broken, it is almost impossible to win back. That is why integrity is not an accessory to character. It is the core.

The West Point Cadet Honor Code states simply: "A Cadet will not lie, cheat, steal, or tolerate those who do." It was first formalized under General Douglas MacArthur, and it is a single sentence that can be applied in every corner of life. The US Army value of integrity expands on it:

> Do what's right, legally and morally. Integrity is a quality you develop by adhering to moral principles. It requires that you do and say nothing that deceives others. As your integrity grows, so does the trust others place in you. The more choices you make based on integrity, the more this highly prized value will affect your relationships with family and friends, and, finally, the fundamental acceptance of yourself.

These are not lofty ideals. They are daily guardrails.

Integrity is not only military doctrine. It is one of the Ten Commandments: "Thou shalt not bear false witness against your neighbor" (Exodus 20:16). The Ten Commandments do not explicitly say "Thou shalt not lie," but this commandment has always been understood as a prohibition against lying. The same principle appears in almost every religion and in nearly every cultural interpretation of morality. All traditions recognize that without truth and honesty, no society can endure.

What begins as memorization has to become more than a soldier's creed. It has to transfer into personal identity. It has to become part of the answer to the question, Who am I? The right answer is simple: I am someone who can be trusted. I am someone who has a moral code.

In Iraq, I saw how the tests of integrity never stopped. They came in many forms. A truck stacked with gold bars that lured one soldier to steal. A briefcase of cash pushed into my hands on a roadside, a bribe offered when only my RTO was close enough to see what choice I would make. Even the barrels we chose to light up as a weapons check carried their own temptation—not in firing them but in owning the result. When the explosion created a mushroom cloud visible for miles, the easy path would have been to deny it or shift blame. Instead, I had to key the radio and admit, yes, that was us. Each moment was different, but the test was the same.

Integrity is not something you can set aside in a moment and expect to pick up later without consequence. It is both ironclad and fragile. When it is whole, it can resist any temptation or doubt. When it is broken, it becomes delicate, and the smallest crack can spread into lasting damage. Humans make mistakes, and in some cases trust can be rebuilt, but integrity is different. It can be lost in an instant and take months or years to restore, if it can be restored at all. The soldier who stole from the gold truck carried that choice with him from that day forward. Had I taken the bribe, even quietly, my men would have known I could be bought. And if I had denied responsibility for the mushroom cloud, the sky itself would have revealed the truth.

Integrity can be tested in silence, with only one set of eyes on you, or with no eyes at all. It can be tested in the open, when everyone is watching. The result has to be the same every time. It should be ironclad. Never questioned. Never lost. And once broken, like that mushroom cloud rising into the sky, it can never be pulled back down.

CHAPTER 9

THE COLONEL OF BUCHA

YOU KNOW HOW IT IS: married couple, two busy careers, lots of travel, three kids; you have to grab any quiet minute to trade updates. "Honey," I beckoned. "Soccer pickup is now at four. The car guy has to special order your starter solenoid, and Isabel needs her TB booster for camp. Oh, and Liam and I are putting together a research hop for next week. Like, maybe ten days in Europe."

"Where in Europe?"

"Poland and Ukraine."

Right away she gave me that look.

It was April 2022, two months after Russia had launched the largest ground attack in Europe since World War II. They had tried to seize Kyiv but were driven back. In a small way, I had helped the defenders, and I wanted to keep my finger on the pulse. But this wasn't 1954, Sarah wasn't a shrinking housewife, and I wasn't sneaking off to a sales conference.

"John, State and DOD have Ukraine at Level 4. That means, 'Don't go.'"

"We're not going under flag. It's just me and Liam. Two random dudes seeing the sights."

She brought up Google Maps. "Show me where."

I pointed vaguely, one of those moments I wished I had married a pastry chef instead of an Army officer.

"And where are the Russians at this point?"

"Basically Belarus."

She fretted some more. "John, if you ever got picked up over there...and they figured out who you are. They'll say you guys are CIA. You'll be in a gulag until you're old and gray."

I put my arm around her waist. "Babe, have you ever known me to do something stupid?"

She faced me, traced a fingertip down my bad ear. "Never."

It was true we'd be bucking US travel advisories. On the other hand, I am one of the foremost experts on urban warfare, and Ukraine's rout of Putin's hordes from their capital city was inarguably the most significant battle of the century. Liam and I had been glued to every available newsfeed for eight weeks; now we needed to see it with our own eyes. Walk the ground, interview the defenders. Survey their tactics, equipment, and conditions. This is where my life and career has taken me, and I do it with pride.

You don't just waltz into a war-torn nation. Air travel was heavily restricted, the trains in and out of neighboring countries booked solid. Which left driving. As a former defense advisory staffer to Ukraine, Liam knew who to tap for support. We cofounded West Point's Modern War Institute. He served as the founding director, a former Special Forces officer with a PhD, and a world-class athlete, to boot. If you're heading down the River Styx, he's the boatman you want.

We flew to Warsaw, where a contact arranged a car to get us to the Ukrainian border. The driver didn't need to cross. He let us out just shy of the checkpoint. We had picked one of two crossings we thought might attract less attention, but as you might imagine, two American pedestrians with backpacks walking through a vehicle lane did the opposite. The border guard dubiously studied our passports, then our faces, then our passports again.

"Where you go?" he asked.

"Ukraine."

He gave us a look that said, "Yes, and?"

"Lviv," we answered.

His buddy asked the same, got the same reply, then said, "Wait here."

A few minutes later, things got strange. The guards motioned us toward a faded Skoda sedan, inside of which were four women, the trunk full of grocery sacks. The guards spoke with them, indicating us, and the women's eyes went wide. They argued, then relented, and the guards motioned for Liam and me to get in. The upshot was clear: We couldn't enter on foot, only by vehicle—any vehicle.

Dismayed, the women shoved groceries aside. We stowed our packs as gently as we could, squeezed in, and did our best to smile and say thanks. They ignored us; the driver's hands clenched the wheel. When the guards finally waved us through, one woman turned suspiciously. "Where you go?"

"Lviv," Liam replied, and her eyes went wide. Did she think we wanted them to take us all the way there? Thankfully, I had been texting a contact I had made in the Ministry of Defense, who reported that our young Ukrainian driver, Fedir, was parked on the Ukrainian side of the border. When we saw him waving, Liam tapped our driver's shoulder. We'd never seen four ladies happier to be rid of us.

Driving to Lviv that evening and our first four hours on the road to Kyiv the next morning offered no further drama. Lots of checkpoints, but no real signs of battle. A few missile strikes aside, Russia had not attacked this far west, and most of the rural Ukraine we saw recalled the endless American Midwest plains Liam and I both hail from. Approaching the outskirts of the capital, though, things grew more ominous. Damaged buildings. Burned-out cars and vans along the highway. Road signs either removed or painted over, part of the effort to frustrate the invaders. Endless lines at the few gas stations still in business.

We understood the big picture of recent events. Instead of cowering as Russian parade-ready columns rolled in to assume power, the city's leaders instead coordinated with military planners, then mobilized civilian volunteers to prepare a latticework of defensive positions, all designed to herd the invaders into narrow, vulnerable corridors of approach. Frustrated at every setback, bottled up until their superior numbers became a liability, the Russians suffered a classic defeat at the hands of a far smaller, less-equipped enemy, much as the ancient Persians were famously thwarted by three hundred Spartans.

Around Kyiv, there was no single grand clash. The battle unfolded across hundreds of square miles, with numerous medium- and small-scale engagements. We had several locations we wanted to inspect, and Bucha was first on our list.

By the time we arrived, Bucha had already become a name whispered in horror. Russian soldiers tied Ukrainian men, women, children, and the elderly with their hands bound behind their backs, then slaughtered them at close range. Some were shot point-blank, others execution style. The images emerging from the town were not war—they were evil. A special kind of evil.

This was not the kind of violence Liam and I, hardened by conflict, had seen before. This was intimate murder, cruelty close up, and for that reason in its own way even worse. The somber truth was still being uncovered: Videos would surface later, mass graves would be exhumed, and stories of torture, mutilation, and sexual assault would flood the world.

Authorities recovered hundreds of bodies after Russian forces withdrew. The local count eventually rose to 458 in Bucha alone, most of them shot and many with binding marks on their hands.

A mass grave, about a forty-five-foot trench near St. Andrew and All Saints Church, held a dozen or more bodies in body bags when satellite imagery first revealed it. Entire families were found in their homes, their lives extinguished in what local testimonies later described as acts of systemic terror. Seventeen bodies were found in a mass grave just days after we visited, among the earliest grim confirmations that what was happening in Bucha was only beginning to be fully known. The full number would climb later.

This northeastern exurb was the first place we landed. The first unit we met wore a mix of military and civilian wear, led by a fearsome giant of a man with an enormous bald head. They called him the Colonel. He was a mountain of a man. When he shook my hand, mine vanished inside his grip. His hands were like ham hocks, the kind of grip that warned you not to trifle with him.

Like most older Ukrainian men, he had served in the Soviet Army. Service was mandatory, and the state conscripted them all, training them to fight for Moscow's interests whether they wanted to or not. That was the one piece missing from the popular movie *Red Dawn.* Teenagers may go "Wolverine" when invaded, but in the real world it is the veterans of the community who rise. They may have been drafted into an empire's army years before, but now, when their own streets and families are threatened, that training, combined with their anger and determination, becomes the backbone of resistance. That is the real *Red Dawn*, and that is exactly what happened in Ukraine.

The Colonel's unit was not part of the Ukrainian regular army, but a Community Defense Force. Groups like his had effectively tripled Kyiv's defensive strength, filling the gaps with citizen-soldiers who brought their experience, their resolve, and their rage into the fight.

The Colonel's men had endured two months of horror and had little patience for another dog-and-pony show. But when our guide introduced me as "Major Spencer, the man who wrote the manual," the Colonel's eyes lit up. Pumping my hand in gratitude, he rallied his men, sang my praises, and they broke out in appreciative whistles, cheers, and applause. I felt like Tom Cruise, only it wasn't my looks or daring that these citizen-soldiers admired. It was my Twitter feed.

That was how I brought my urban warfare experience to bear from half a world away.

It began on Day 3 of the invasion. The Ukrainian government, as well as the city of Kyiv, had directed all citizens to resist. Which was great, but try as I might, I could not find any public information the Ukrainian people could access to explain *how* they should resist a modern army.

So my thumbs went to work. I began by tweeting commonsense self-protection most soldiers would be familiar with but would likely be news to the uninitiated. Then I went into the specifics of area fortifying, obstructing the enemy's progress, and the basics of movement, attack, and evasion. It's a compendium of the wisdom I've accrued and imparted to my classes at West Point in my public speaking engagements, articles, and TV commentary.

My tweets blew up. Went viral. Word filtered back that Ukrainian leaders from all walks of life were printing out my bullet points, collecting them in packets, and distributing them. The Ukrainian government translated and posted my information on their official Ministry of Defense website for resisters. Soon enough, I did the same: self-publishing a mini manual on do-it-yourself urban warfare for defenders. It's now available in seventeen languages, and you can download it for free on my website. I've enjoyed my share of glories and laurels, but becoming a go-to guy during a partner nation's darkest hours, their fight for freedom, will undoubtedly stand as my most fulfilling professional achievement.

Our new friend, the Colonel of Bucha, now treated us like dignitaries, inviting us to inspect his men, their weapons, and happily recounting his unit's actions. He was an outstanding field officer, who four months earlier had been managing an electronics shop. And as Liam and I toured other battle areas in the coming days, we met dozens of men and women just like him. Regular people who buckled down when every expert predicted their nation was toast. They committed themselves to dare the impossible, then worked together tirelessly to make it happen. Putin's show troops never stood a chance, and the reserves, convicts, mercenaries, and conscripts he continues to send have fared little better.

None of which should suggest our visit was some kind of victory lap. Liam and I both have extensive combat experience. We've seen every damage the human body can suffer, the destruction wrought upon families, communities, and nations. War is not something you get used to. Around Kyiv, we stood in meadows, alleys, and back lots where massacres occurred, and you don't need a guide to tell you that even after the bodies are removed, the stench of death lingers. You taste it in the air, feel it in your gut. And every wrecked car we saw, every destroyed house, collapsed building, or churned-up field had belonged to somebody. I don't cry on hearing every new horror, but it all goes into a giant notebook in my head called *What Putin's Done.*

As a dad, it's the faces of the children that get me now. They're never front and center on a trip like ours, but always on the periphery; a few excited by all the upheaval and adventure, but too many seemingly in shock from all they've witnessed. Are they refugees? Hungry? Orphaned? Every haunted face hides a unique and usually tragic story. Some we heard; most we didn't. When the sadness weighs on me heavily, I go back to the foundational reason I became a soldier, why I continue to study and promote best military practices: I am a defender by nature. I want to see as few lives devastated as possible, and a true warrior devotes their life to minimizing the cruelty and destructive power of the world's aggressors. And the great victory of Kyiv is that the losses and destruction could easily have been ten times worse.

I also don't want to imply my "celebrity" status provided us some kind of magical force field. Thanks to Liam and some of the new associates I had met while evolving my manual, we were shepherded about by some of the best and brightest in Ukrainian defense. But trauma, miscommunication, and fear can easily erupt into a bad scene.

Among the brilliant but unsung tacticians of the Ukrainian defense were civil engineers. Kyiv's three hundred square miles are crisscrossed by dams and rivers, and the military realized they could selectively flood the lowlands most likely to be used by Russian ground forces. It doesn't take a great deal of standing water to turn land or streams into rivers, with blown bridges made impassable for heavy vehicles. Entire columns were thus confronted by obstacles not indicated on their maps, and Russians are poorly trained to adapt to changing conditions. Confounded, the invaders fell back on the most obvious alternative: using roads, some of which the Ukrainians had helpfully left open and clear. Elated, Russian tanks and support vehicles went zooming down these optimal surfaces, making up for all the time lost in unexpected mud, and their jubilation lasted until the moment they drove into extensively prepared Ukrainian kill zones, ambush sites from which there was no escape. In one instance, a Russian column of a hundred vehicles was hoping to cross a still-intact bridge over the Bucha River when they came under fire by concealed Ukrainian forces. The fuel truck bringing up the rear of the parade was the first to erupt in flames, then the vehicles at the very front, leaving everyone trapped in between. Nothing survived the ensuing turkey shoot. It was engagements like this throughout the city's outskirts that hobbled Russia's numerical superiority.

For most of the trip, we had a high-level escort from Ukraine's Ministry of Defense. She understood our mission was not tourism, but research. We weren't there for photo opportunities; we wanted to understand why the Russians had failed, and why the Ukrainians had succeeded. We were looking for the decisive factors, both in terrain and in human stories. Battles often turn on such details, and a single feature of ground or a single leader's decision can alter the course of a war.

But our guide had her own duties to attend to as well. One evening when she had to leave us, Liam and I decided we would try to fit in one last site before the day ended. We asked our driver to take us to Moschun, a small village on the periphery of the capital that had been the scene of a massive fight. There, the Russians had come dangerously close to breaking through Ukrainian defenses.

When we arrived, we found local soldiers still guarding the ruins. We asked what questions we could, piecing together fragments of their story. They pointed us toward the places where Russian forces had tried to ford the Irpin River, places where the defenders had fought desperately to hold them back. A few farmers gestured "over there," so we pressed farther on by car. Soon the paved road gave way to dirt. After a while we noticed that we were driving on ground where there were no more tire tracks. Our driver grew visibly nervous. "Not good," he muttered. "Mines."

The message was clear. Liam and I nodded in agreement, and he put the car in reverse. Slowly, carefully, we backed out the way we had come, keeping our wheels exactly inside our own tracks. Nobody spoke much until we had rolled back onto the road. The silence said enough. It reminded us we were not sightseeing, but researching how battles turned. Every place we went carried the imprint of choices that shaped the battle. Moschun had been one of those places where defenders held at terrible cost, and we wanted to see the next: the deliberate flooding that had altered the very ground under the invaders.

The next morning our regular guide was still occupied, and her replacement arrived. He was a capable if blustery senior army officer assigned to escort us on our final day. Liam and I wanted to inspect various flood zones on the Irpin River, marveling at the precision with which Ukrainian engineers had planned and executed this unprecedented use of natural resources. They had not flooded at random. They had opened or blown dam gates in a coordinated effort upstream, turning rivers into weapons to slow or block the Russian advance.

We stopped on one bridge that afforded the best view of a breached dam. In front of us was the flooded village of Demydiv, its houses, fields, and lowlands submerged by water pushed in from the dam breach. The inundation there had been deliberate, a defensive measure to deny Russian vehicles an entire approach to the capital city and to force them into choke points.

Standing on that road, looking across the drowned terrain, you could see how the deliberate flooding had reshaped the battlefield. What had once been passable land now lay under water, a barrier where there had once been roads. As we stood making notes and taking pictures, one of the Ukrainian guards at the scene started shouting. It was clear he had orders not to allow survey of the wreckage, and he was moving in our direction at a fast pace. His weapon remained slung, but his hands rested on it in a way that put Liam and me instantly on alert. I would later learn that Liam, ever cautious, had quietly tossed his phone into the car in anticipation of having it confiscated. We laugh about it now, but at the time it was a "thanks, buddy" moment, as I stood there with my phone still in my hand.

The soldier continued toward us, shouting. We gestured our willingness to move on, but our new escort had other ideas. He shouted back, authoritative and defiant. Whatever he claimed, the guard did not back down. His rifle came off his shoulder as he closed on us in rising fury. Liam and I exchanged glances. The guard was a teenager, likely with little or no training, just orders. Our guide's face turned red as he cursed back. He was also armed, a handgun visible on his waist.

Back and forth they shouted, the muzzle of the boy's rifle rising inch by inch. We waited helplessly, praying for things to de-escalate. Only after several anxious minutes did our guide finally motion us back to the vehicles. Even then I was sure we would be detained. Slowly, we drove off, and only once safely across did we start breathing normally again. Thankfully, that was our closest call with unfriendly friendlies, nor did we come close enough to any Russian units to risk encounter. Which is perhaps why we decided to push our luck. The engineers' work at Demydiv had shown us how terrain could become a weapon. To complete the picture, we needed to study how the Russians had tried to withdraw and how the Ukrainians turned even that retreat into another battlefield. That search took us north toward Ivankiv.

The only military feat the Russians performed with professional skill was their retreat from Kyiv. Utterly rebuffed and decimated in their efforts to breach the heart of the capital, they finally turned tail for the long, lonely rural roads back to their staging grounds inside Belarus. The Ukrainians harassed them every step of the way with artillery, drones, and raids. One rally point the Russians used to cover their retreat was the suburb of Ivankiv, northeast of the capital and midway to the border, where they dug tank fighting positions directly into the highway itself. After inspecting those abandoned positions, we continued north along the trail of dead machines that had never made it. Some of the wrecks had been cleared, but many still waited, piles of useless molten slag. Our driver, young Fedir, seemed to grow more and more uneasy the farther north we went.

After a few more miles we discovered the source of Fedir's uneasiness. We slowed for a rural traffic circle in the middle of which stood a billboard with a large yellow-and-black nuclear symbol and the words *Chernobyl-tour.UA*. That was odd. How close were we to the most notorious industrial accident in modern history?

I turned to Liam. "Are we close to Chernobyl?"

"Must be."

"Well, how close is it?"

We both checked our Google Maps, but the service was not working.

We asked Fedir. He gestured ahead. "Not far, up there." Which could have meant anything. We pressed on. The land looked unchanged, with fields, forest, and distant hills, but there were no fences or warning signs. We kept our eyes peeled for living Russians, not radioactive zombies. Liam and I remembered following reports of the Russian advance on Kyiv and how Chernobyl had suddenly reappeared in the news. I had asked, "Chernobyl is in Ukraine?" and Liam had been quick to quip, "Yes, John, it was in the Soviet Union in Ukraine."

Now we were experiencing firsthand how, ahead of the Russian advance, the Ukrainians had removed every road sign possible, including everything related to the nuclear power plant that had melted down in 1986 and turned everything in a twenty-mile radius into a contaminated no-go zone. Chernobyl happened to sit alongside this same road to Belarus, and stories circulated widely about Russian infantry who had unknowingly halted inside the danger zone. Had they just stood around, they might have been fine. But as soldiers tend to do come nightfall, they dug foxholes near the plant, and some quickly became sick from the radioactive particles in the soil. How many succumbed, were evacuated, or eventually died will likely never be known. I could not help but wonder how many rads we were absorbing just driving through the area.

Not much farther up, our guide, whose car we had been following, stopped, explained the last attacks of the retreating Russians at that spot, and through his window bid us farewell. He pointed us to the road left, which skirted the Belarusian border all the way west back to Poland. Liam and I knew it was over a six-hour drive, so we agreed we should take care of business before we started. We popped our doors and stepped off the road. As I lingered over a bush, I could hear Fedir panicking in the car. I could not fathom why at first, but he was terrified of Chernobyl's radiation. Liam and I wasted no time, climbed back in, and the moment we did, Fedir sped off like we had just robbed a bank.

Fedir drove as if he were in the Indy 500. At first, we thought his panic came only from Chernobyl, but we soon realized it was something else entirely—it was the proximity of Belarus that had him terrified. To him, danger was not theoretical radiation but the very real border with Belarus and whatever might come across it. That fear made him push the car to reckless speed on an unimproved highway, hitting giant potholes at more than seventy miles an hour. Liam and I still say the greatest danger we ever faced in Ukraine was on that country road with no cell phone coverage, just waiting for one of those bone-jarring hits to a pothole to cause either our death outright or a breakdown that would leave us stranded, vulnerable to whatever found us.

With our nerves blown, we finally reached the same Ukraine-Poland border crossing we had entered through. We walked across, relieved to be out of that car.

Back home in Colorado, my Uber driver was super chatty. "Look at this traffic. They got half the roads shut down for 'beautification projects,' but who can smell any flowers at forty miles per hour? And seriously, another brew pub? All these people got nothing better to do?"

He eased to a stop at my driveway. "You got the bags? I threw out my back last week."

As he drove away, I stood for a moment, pondering. We had seen so much over there, and I knew my wife would have a million questions.

I figured it was best I just skip the whole Chernobyl part.

LESSON: SERVICE

Service is the act of helping or working for someone beyond yourself. One of the US Army's core values, selfless service, teaches: "Put the welfare of the nation, the Army and your subordinates before your own. Selfless service is larger than just one person. In serving your country, you are doing your duty loyally without thought of recognition or gain. The basic building block of selfless service is the commitment of each team member to go a little further, endure a little longer, and look a little closer to see how he or she can add to the effort."

That value captured what I saw in Bucha and what I have seen in other war zones. Service means putting something greater than yourself first. When your family, your community, or your nation is under attack, when freedom, yours or someone else's, is threatened, or when there is a bully (and I hate bullies), you stand up. To serve is to step forward.

We are tribal by biology. Every person needs a family, a tribe, a community, a nation. Serving those beyond yourself is both a commitment and an expression of belonging.

The Colonel of Bucha embodied this truth. He had every reason to stay home. He was no longer a professional soldier. Yet when the invasion came, he stepped forward, bringing his strength, his training, and his resolve. That was his service to his neighbors, to his town, and to his country. And he was not alone. Across Ukraine, ordinary people did the same. Their service multiplied into a force strong enough to stop an empire. On every visit I felt it, people serving one another so they could be free, so they could live free.

I also had my own role to play. I was not Ukrainian, but I carried knowledge few others possessed. Writing the manual and pushing it out to anyone who could use it was my way of serving. It was not for recognition or gain. It was simply doing my part because I could, because I must. It was an extension of my identity as a soldier and a scholar. I am proud that the manual helped thousands, that it was seen across Ukraine, from Lviv to Mariupol, and that it was translated and used as far away as Iran and Myanmar, in places I sometimes heard about but could never fully know.

That is the truth of life, in or out of uniform. Families, friends, communities, and nations endure when people serve. No free-loading. No shrinking back. Each of us has a way to serve and to strengthen the lives of others. And, in turn, that service becomes a defining part of our character.

CHAPTER 10

HIGH ON A MOUNTAIN TOP

THE YEAR AFTER THAT WAS pretty bad. Good professionally, but my marriage came to an end. It was my third, my longest-lasting, and it ran our three school-age kids through the wringer.

It was a year when I really appreciated the people who truly cared about me, the ones who were more than friends, who had become family. I wound up having a lot of dark-night-of-the-soul conversations with my old buddy Leon Hall. I'd grown up without a father or any paternal presence, and he was the first unit leader to take me under his wing at Fort Polk, Louisiana. I was eighteen; he was three years older. He started out as my team leader, became my teacher, counselor, guru, and all-around Jiminy Cricket. Leon knew what to say and when silence mattered more. As far as listening goes, he went above and beyond that year.

"If I could do it all over," I sighed at one point, "I guess I would've been around more."

He gave that some space. He's been around the block himself. "Well, John," he finally drawled softly, "at least we know you've survived worse."

That got a grim smile out of me.

He was talking about Ranger School, the most grueling advanced training course ever devised by the US Army. I did it when I was twenty, and Leon happened to be there as well.

The average soldier does not seek out opportunities to push their mind and body to the absolute breaking point. A standard Army enlistment is three years, which most recruits regard as a respectable first step into adulthood, a chance to earn some money, and gain maturity, skills, and experience they can apply to a decent civilian job. Others aspire to a military career in the many service and support branches that are less dependent on physical readiness. Then there are the warriors who gravitate to the combat arms, filling the ranks of the Army's infantry, tank, artillery, and helicopter units. Then there are kids like me who aspire to be the fighting elite and obsessively pursue any chance for a coveted slot at the Ranger or Special Forces Schools. Those who pass Ranger School get to wear the Ranger tab on their shoulder for the rest of their career, which is like a flashing neon sign that tells everyone in the military you've proven yourself under the most severe conditions. There's a famous quote by Colonel "Tex" Turner: "I woke up in a cold sweat. I'd had a nightmare that I was back in Ranger School. Thank God I was in Vietnam. Compared to Ranger School, combat was easy."

That was a test I wanted to pass, and I was under no illusions about what I was getting into. Only about 38 percent of candidates graduate on their first try. Those who wash out can go back and restart the course from Day 1, or repeat the different phases, but even among these "recycles," only about half make it. The course is simply too demanding. Beyond the obvious strength and fitness requirements, candidates get an average of zero to four hours of sleep per night. The rest of the time you are on your feet, most likely walking. Food wise, you get one or two Army MRE (meals ready to eat) rations per day. That might sound like plenty since an MRE contains around 1,500 calories, but it is no exaggeration to say a Ranger student, moving twenty or more hours a day, can burn over 5,000 calories daily.

In the real world, you could handle a work schedule like that for a few days at best.

Ranger School is *sixty-two* days.

The first four days at Fort Benning, Georgia, are like the regular Army. You sleep in barracks, eat at the chow hall, and complete a series of physical fitness tests. It was there in the parking lot I spotted a man who looked so familiar being dropped off by a taxi.

"Sergeant Hall!"

He turned and welcomed me with a big grin. It was about a year and a half since I'd left Fort Polk, where the two of us spent weeks at a time manning "enemy" patrol bases during war game exercises. As it turned out, we'd now been assigned to start the same Ranger class. Once we started, we learned we would be in different companies of the same course, so we wouldn't see much of each other, but just knowing Sergeant Hall was close by upped my resolve to take everything they tried to dish out. I had no father in my life, but Leon had already filled that space more than once. Seeing him there reminded me I wasn't walking this road alone.

Candidates who pass the tough physical and mental tests of the first week spend the rest of Phase 1 living in the woods, without tents, performing back-to-back small unit missions like ambushes, raids, and reconnaissance patrols. You take turns rotating in and out of the leadership positions while steely-eyed Ranger instructors scrutinize your every move and decision. This represented my first hurdle. Most Ranger School candidates are either officers or veteran sergeants: men trained in the planning of complex operations and issuing Army-standard orders. I was just a grunt, and a kid to boot, and if I had to play catch-up and learn how to do a leader's job on the fly, it was all on me.

Living outdoors is a quick reminder how civilization has eased the human condition. Three days in the field with scant food and sleep was already debilitating, then I discovered a new weakness: my ability to fall asleep at the drop of a hat. If I dozed off and got left behind, though, I'd earn demerits or even get kicked out. So I started coming up with little tricks, like munching on raw coffee grounds or plucking my facial hairs just for the little jolt of pain.

Luckily, I had a superpower as well: I've always been able to carry a lot of weight. I'm not a giant or a bodybuilder; I think it comes from growing up poor and walking for miles across town to visit my grandmother almost every damn day since I was little. A good mule also takes the load off others, so I was betting my grateful colleagues would shake me awake when it was time to stagger on.

Not everyone was so blessed. The greatest number of dropouts came during orientation: guys who couldn't do enough push-ups, run five miles, or find points in the woods at night on the land-nav test. Every day in the field, one or two more of our hopefuls bit the dust. You can choose to leave any time, the instructors can kick you out, or guys who come off like jerks can get voted off the island by their peers. There's zero downtime to make friends; what little small talk is exchanged is mostly devoted to the food people wished they had.

"Clams casino."

"Venison jerky."

"Hostess Sno Balls."

I didn't add much to those discussions. When you've known food scarcity as a kid and stood in line for hours for a block of government cheese, even Army chow seems pretty darn tasty.

Three weeks later, we were gifted what seemed like a real break: a two-week vacation. Our class had started in November, so we got Christmas off. My mom drove down to pick me up, squinting in puzzlement when she saw I'd already lost a dozen pounds. I crawled into the back seat of her car, stinking from weeks without clean clothes or a shower, and slept the entire ten-hour drive back to Indiana. At first it seemed great, sleeping twelve hours a day, sharing meals with my two grown sisters. To them, I was echelons above reality—a man who knew what he wanted, then departed their world so completely it was like I'd hopped a space shuttle. The more I vegged out, though, the more I realized this interlude was more of a curse than a blessing: The best way to run a gauntlet is to barrel straight on through. Stopping midstream only made the dread of starting up again that much worse.

Ranger School, Phase 2, is the mountain course. It again started with a few days in the classroom. Then the doors opened, and we gazed up at the surrounding snowy peaks of Georgia's Chattahoochee–Oconee National Forest. The first assignment is simple: *Get your ass up there!*

Hiking northern Georgia in December isn't bad, but once you pass the snowline, it's a different story. We were carrying jackets and Gore-Tex long johns, but you can't actually wear heavy layers during physical exertion because you'll start pouring sweat, overheat, and pass out. All we had for the cold were gloves with no inserts and boots with regular socks. After six or seven hours that day, sometimes on slopes so steep we were on hands and knees, I started wondering when they'd call it a day. And once we got wherever we were going, what would we find? They couldn't just let us drop up here; the minute we stopped moving, we'd freeze. Just a year before, four candidates had died of hypothermia in the course—the worst disaster in Ranger School history. Now we regretted taking those two weeks off even more. We'd all gone soft, and whatever lay ahead wasn't going to be cookies and hot chocolate.

I was starting to get seriously worried. I knew all the warning signs: brain fog, slurred speech, sluggish movements. I had all three, and all I could hope was that no one else had noticed and that the coming nightfall meant we were nearly done.

Then it started raining.

Raining drops that stung like shots from a pellet gun because they were already turning to ice. The downpour became a storm, and still we trudged on and up like zombies until I knew I'd climbed as high as I possibly could. Indiana's winters were not enough to prepare me; you can't train yourself to not be cold. All I could picture were the four men who succumbed last year, and I strongly suspected I'd soon be joining them. This was where my dreams had led me.

Here lies John Spencer, fallen at Ranger School.

And then we hit a crest. If not the tip-top, it was at least a plateau, and through the trees we could see in the moonlight a large tent with a vehicle parked nearby. Getting closer, we saw the red cross on a white field. It was an ambulance to carry away our half-dead.

"Don't be shy, studs," the attending medical officer announced. "Anybody wants a nice ride back down to Camp Merrill, you'll be all toasty and warm."

Like oxen, some guys staggered toward him, our beautiful, merciful savior, but I heard a tiny, cracked voice in my head: "This is how they do it, man! Break you down, then dangle a ray of comfort just to see if you'll throw away the weeks you've endured...because the only place that ambulance is taking you is back to Day 1."

Resolved, I stayed with the non-quitters. They halted us at the tent. "Weatherman says it's five below," an RI said. "So we're gonna spoil you. Keep you out of the wind 'til sunup."

It was our final Christmas miracle. For me, though, it was too little, too late.

I knew I'd had it. Had to get off that mountain ASAP, or I was done for. The ice storm was just my final stroke of rotten luck. I'd have to go back and start over. Was I crying as I turned away, letting the rest file in past me? I couldn't feel a thing. On the verge of passing out, I moved mechanically toward the ambulance when a familiar figure suddenly stood in my path.

"Nice night for a walk."

It was Sergeant Hall. Trying to smile through his grimace.

"In a winter wonderland," I rasped.

"Where you headed, John?"

I tried to swallow. Nodded toward the ambulance.

"Yeah? You sure about that?"

Shame welled up inside me, and it felt a *lot* worse than hypothermia.

He gave my shoulder an encouraging jab. "You can always quit tomorrow." That was not just a Ranger line but it was the kind of fatherly wisdom I had never had growing up passed to me at the exact moment I needed it most.

I slowly nodded. Tapping my last ounce of strength, I about-faced, and we took shelter.

I'd like to say that night was the worst, but mountain phase never got any better. Cold-weather injuries and fatigue abounded, guys dropped out left and right, but I pushed on. No hypothermia, but chilblain is no picnic either, which is when your hands and feet swell up and blister from the cold and damp. When Phase 2 finally ended, we were dropped into Phase 3.

By parachute.

There's nothing like a refreshing dip in the ol' swimmin' hole, and the Army's version of that is the rank swamps of Florida's Eglin Air Force Base. There we resumed our wall-to-wall missions: long-range patrols, setting up ambushes, conducting raids, digging two-man fighting positions for the sleep we were never going to get.

"Ribeye steak."

"Pot pie."

"Gray snail."

"What's that?"

"When the bartender announces last call, tell him to detach that metal tray that runs along his side. Have him tilt it so all the spillage from the night pours into a glass. That's a gray snail."

Some problems from the mountain remained. A number of guys had frostnip, the early onset of frostbite. With proper foot care, you fully recover, but wading through muck up to your thighs is *not* proper foot care. People quickly found that trench foot on top of frostnip was making their feet blow up like balloons. Some guys had pain so intense it felt like they were walking on broken glass. Men of unquenchable fire who'd lasted for forty or fifty days simply could not walk ten steps. But the rules were the rules. If you can't hack Day 48, back to Day 1 you go.

Somehow I was still in the game. Got lucky again when I was assigned my leadership position as a squad leader on an ambush. A squad is the smallest Army unit, a dozen men tops, and I'd been on dozens of ambush drills as a regular soldier. I thought I acquitted myself well, but you never know for sure because the instructors never tell you your grades.

Meanwhile, more men fell out with foot pain. Seeing their faces as the stretchers carried them off was heartbreaking and never more so than when I went to the weekly religious service offered to Rangers in the middle of the swamp. There was Sergeant Hall, and just seeing him gave me a burst of energy. But when I greeted him, he hung his head in near tears. His feet were so swollen he was wearing boots two sizes bigger, but that wasn't enough to quell the pain.

"I guess it just wasn't meant to be," he muttered.

"Well, Sarge, uh, y'know. . . ."

He looked up sharply. "What?"

"You can always quit tomorrow."

He stared at me long and hard.

Then, holding a tree for support, he hauled himself to his feet. "I'll walk you out, John."

It was my turn to steady him, the way family does. That moment sealed it for me. He was no longer just my sergeant. He was my brother.

His face was so red from holding it in I thought he was going to burst. But he didn't quit that day. Or the next. And then, miraculously, his pains largely subsided, and he carried on.

"My grandpappy's homemade *golabki* with red sauce."

"Scrambled eggs with basil, tomato, and smoked salmon."

"The all-you-can-eat buffet at Ponderosa."

I felt like telling them what my mom used to tell me: "If you're hungry, go to sleep."

Then, somehow, it was all over.

About half of us who started were still alive and kicking.

Back at Fort Benning, we had a day off before the graduation ceremony, and a bunch of us actually went to Ponderosa. We had all lost about thirty pounds and looked like we had escaped from a concentration camp. Smelled like it too. After months of living on minimal calories, our bodies could not handle a lot of food, and every man at our table wound up violently ill.

I recovered just enough to get through graduation. It was all worth it, I decided, rubbing that sacred Ranger tab between my fingers. A fairly tiny patch, just six yellow letters on a black arch with a yellow border, but I had never been prouder of anything in my life.

The following morning as I crossed the same parking lot where I had first reunited with Sergeant Hall, I spotted him again, stowing his gear into a taxi. Elated, I hurried over.

"What is your next post?" I asked. He looked as gaunt as I did.

"Doc says to stay off my feet," he said with a weary grin. "So the Army put me in for ten weeks of clog dancing."

We laughed and shook hands. "Take care of yourself, Sergeant."

"You too, my brother."

He had never called me that before, but it felt right. We had walked through the valley of the shadow of death together, and he was no longer just a leader or mentor. He was family.

It is hard to believe that was almost thirty years ago. Leon served more than three decades, rising to colonel in senior command planning. More importantly, after all these years, he is still my brother.

Still my family.

LESSON: FAMILY

Family is blood, of course, but it is not exclusive to blood. The truth is bigger than that.

Family is found wherever people choose to walk through the fire together, refusing to quit on one another.

That is the real lesson.

No one is meant to go through life alone. We all need people who steady us when we stumble and remind us that we can endure. When Leon told me, "You can always quit tomorrow," it was more than a Ranger line. It was wisdom given at the exact moment I needed it most.

I tell my kids often that we have priorities in life: family, school, friends, sports. Family comes first. A true member of a family is someone who will be there for you through thick and thin, who will sacrifice their time or drop everything to help out of love. That can be blood family, or it can be the family you find in mentors, friends, and teammates.

Over the years, Leon became a mentor, a father figure, and a brother. That bond was forged at Fort Polk, Louisiana, through Ranger School, but also through life. My kids have heard me talking to Leon, to Liam, or to a few others, and they would hear me call them "brother." When they were young, they would laugh and say, "Dad, you have a lot of brothers." That gave me the chance to explain why we in the military, and in life, use that term. Military members often call each other "brother" or "sister" because the bond forged in service is intense, rooted in trust and shared sacrifice. They are more than close friends. They are truly family. But the essence of that bond is not unique to the military. It can be found anywhere people commit to one another fully, whether in medicine, firefighting, teaching, sports, or any walk of life where people give of themselves for others.

The lesson is that family can be both given and chosen. It is found in those who walk with you through hardship and joy, those who refuse to quit on you, and those you refuse to quit on in return. The challenge is not just to find such people but to be that person yourself. Be a loyal friend, a faithful mentor, a steady hand.

Because the bonds of family, chosen or inherited, are what carry us through the hardest moments.

That is what Leon gave me and what I try to give others. We all need people like that in our lives—and we all have the chance to be that for someone else.

DEFYING GRAVITY II

THE ARMY IS NOT A spectator sport. No tourists at the rifle range, no bring-your-daughter-to-work day, no gift shop. Most of what we do is hidden from view, training behind fences or deploying far from home.

Ironically, one of the most elite programs I had long aspired to was open to spectators. It was the annual Best Ranger Competition, and if there was ever a moment in my career not to make a dumb mistake that almost got me killed, it was there.

But I did.

The Rangers are the Army's best, and the competition was founded in the early eighties as a kind of mini Olympics for Rangers. The selection process begins a year in advance, with roughly a hundred men chosen from across the Army. These competitors are paired into two-person teams, most of whom are excused from their regular duties for the next six months so they can focus entirely on training. The big day arrives each spring at Fort Benning. In reality, it is three days—sixty consecutive hours of mind-body-spirit punishment. No programmed sleep, little food, constant motion. It is designed to break even the strongest.

I was a thirty-year-old captain with back issues when I passed initial team selection in 2007. No one had ever won their very first Best Ranger Competition, and most of my competitors were younger, but there was a thirty-six-year-old major on board, so I was reasonably sure I would not come in dead last. Just finishing is respectable. Most teams do not even make it through the first day.

My partner was Staff Sergeant Simms, a stoic Georgia country boy and family man. He was my equal in every way: physical fitness, weapons proficiency, parachuting, carrying weight over long distances, land navigation, demolitions, field medicine, and obstacle courses. These are skills Rangers perform in their sleep. The challenge of the competition is to perform all of them, flawlessly, one after another, while sleep deprived, half-starved, and pushed past the limits of human endurance. Like Olympic hopefuls, Simms and I trained for efficiency. We shaved every unnecessary thought, movement, and second from our performance times.

On the forty-foot-high cargo net climb, for instance, we figured out you could get back down a lot faster if you didn't jam your boots into the squares. Instead, we curled our legs back toward our butts so they stayed out of the way, hung by our hands alone, and let gravity do most of the work. You dropped fast, braking only with your palms, the rope burning your hands as you controlled the slide. It was like working the rigging on a pirate ship, and Simms and I got so smooth at it we could practically race each other down.

We had practiced that move hundreds of times. It was second nature by the time competition week arrived.

As Day 1 drew closer, my back was good to go. My ankle, unfortunately, was not. "Achilles tendonitis," the doc proclaimed. I was already wearing a steroid patch; now I begged her to inject the stuff straight into the tender flesh. She refused. Too much risk of rupturing the tendon, which would hobble me for life. What was I supposed to do? Stand down? Reapply next year? The thing was: I was not alone. Half the competitors were coming in with injuries. It was inevitable, given the months of training. And, besides, my whole family was coming to watch.

On the morning of, I taped up my lower leg from calf to ankle and reported to the starting line. The kick-off event was a five-mile run to Ranger School's famed Malvestie obstacle course. My ankle was killing me, but at least no one could tell. The strangest part of the day was the civilian cheering section. Parents, grandparents, moms holding up babies. They were not behind fences or seated in bleachers but right there on the sidelines within arm's reach as we crawled through the mud or straddled logs. My mom was in a wheelchair by then, but my sisters maneuvered her along the course, all of them yelling, "Go, Bubba, go!"—my childhood nickname. That moment alone would have made the competition worth it.

Everything was going great for Simms and me until we hit the cargo net climb.

It is basically two telephone poles topped by a cross beam, with the net draped over the beam and hanging vertically on either side. I had climbed a million of them and spent my last six months climbing them really fast, but right away I realized we had a problem.

The course instructors had changed the net.

The new rope was tighter and stiffer. We felt it instantly and adjusted; good soldiers roll with any curveball. I made it to the top, seconds slower than usual, but no big deal. I flipped over the beam, reaching for a handhold, and the weave slipped through my fingers. For a split second I was weightless.

Then the world tilted and the ground came screaming up at my face.

I remember the blur of dirt and iron, the collective gasp of the crowd, the sickening certainty that I was about to die in front of my family. And then—a violent wrench, so sudden it snapped my head back. I dangled in midair, swaying, my face just inches from the Georgia soil.

It took me a moment to understand. My boot. Somehow, impossibly, it had lodged in a single tiny square of rope. That miracle snare had caught me headfirst and held me.

Instructors in black T-shirts and ballcaps were shouting. Horrified civilians gaped. When I craned my neck, I saw Simms still up high, peering down in shock. Then I saw my mom and my sisters a few feet away, their faces ashen. Yeah, I had almost bought it right there in front of them.

Thoughts flew through me. The fragility of life. The odds of coincidence. My purpose in the grand scheme of things. A heartbeat later, I knew my purpose: get clear of this obstacle and sprint like hell to the next one. Freeing my foot, I dropped to the dirt, cursing the points I might be docked. I rolled to my feet, test flexed my back, and yelled up at Simms to get it in gear, then stood there panting until his boots hit the ground.

That was only the morning of Day 1. We still had fifty-nine hours to go.

We did not win the Best Ranger Competition. In fact, we were not even close. I think Simms and I came in tenth place, maybe twelfth. Which is still impressive; of the fifty teams that started, only about twenty dragged themselves over the finish line. Just finishing is an accomplishment, and I was proud of that.

Who actually won the 2007 Best Ranger Competition?

A team made up of two Special Forces soldiers. One was a master sergeant I had served with years earlier in the 2nd Ranger Battalion. The other was a thirty-six-year-old major named Liam Collins. It was his third time competing, and together they took the title.

I barely met Liam that weekend, but some years later I hit him up for a teaching job at West Point. When I pointed out that I had been there to witness his greatest triumph, he laughed. He did not offer me a job. He claims he did not have one at the time. I made it to West Point through a different department than the one Liam was working in then. But we still formed a professional and eventually a personal partnership that has lasted to this day.

So I guess you can say my foot in that net was my foot in the door as well. And, happily, the champ and I remain close colleagues. A brother now. The truth is that it was not my skill or strength that kept me alive that day. It was gravity, luck, and one stubborn boot. Sometimes that is all it takes.

LESSONS: SEE DEFYING GRAVITY III

CHAPTER 11

THE CANARY IN THE COAL MINE

WHEN I PLAYED *MONOPOLY* AS a kid, I always tried to buy up the railroads and utilities, so you can imagine how excited I was in 2003 when I was handed the keys to my first oil refinery. It was in Kirkuk, city center of a major oil-producing region in northern Iraq, but sadly I was no tycoon. I did not own the plant, the land it sat on, the liquid wealth somewhere below it, or the byproducts coursing through the maze of pipes, storage tanks, and separating towers. I was just the US Army platoon leader given responsibility for safeguarding it.

Saddam Hussein's forces had surrendered or scattered to the winds, and the role of the Coalition ground forces shifted to security operations, which frequently means standing watch.

As a hard-charging infantryman, I would rather be on the attack. Taking the initiative, applying my smarts and resources to overcoming the enemy. Guarding stuff? That was defense. Waiting for them to come to you.

Who might be targeting a defeated nation's energy infrastructure?

Our most pressing concern was looters. The minute people saw Saddam's statue pulled down, a crime wave erupted across Iraq, and any property of the state not nailed down was ripe for picking. We saw it all: street gangs filling fleets of pickup trucks with stolen goods, families loading up oxcarts. Left unsupervised, an oil refinery could be stripped clean of any metal or machinery people could turn into quick cash. Thankfully, looters prefer soft targets. Our visible presence in and around the plant would hopefully be enough to dissuade most prowling jackals.

The more insidious threat was sabotage from militants already primed to repulse any foreign presence, especially around their nation's most vital industry. The belief was already out there that we had overthrown Saddam for the express purpose of seizing Iraq's oil, meaning some of the bad guys were determined to go scorched-earth to deny us the "spoils."

I was too young for Desert Storm back in 1991, but the older guys remembered it well. Iraqi forces, routed by Coalition forces across Kuwait, turned their wrath upon the source of their neighbor's wealth and set over six hundred oil wells ablaze. It was an ecological Armageddon and a black eye for the victorious nations. It is wildly hazardous and expensive to snuff out an oil fire, and nobody wanted a repeat of those scenes to play on CNN twelve years later.

Kirkuk had been relatively quiet, but scattered attacks had been reported against pipelines and fuel tankers. Another worry was that, like most infrastructure in Iraq, our plant had been woefully maintained during the decades of Saddam's rule. When Colin Powell warned the president, "If you break it, you're buying it," he was partly referring to the ramshackle condition of the country's power plants, dams, roads, hospitals, and how a suddenly liberated Iraqi people might expect their rich conquerors to get such things up and running again.

So we had plenty of motivation to keep our square mile of heavy industry hassle free.

And it was not like Civil Affairs handed us municipal maps or blueprints of the place. We got our orders, mounted up, drove out to this eyesore, and my captain said, "It's all yours, John."

I studied the dull, gray expanse beyond the fence line. "Do I get an operator's manual?"

"Yeah, please don't touch anything."

And there we were. Forty men, all thrilled about the biggest babysitting job of our lives.

It was true we were not there to run the place, but I definitely wanted to start with an area recon so at least my squad leaders and I would be familiar with the basic layout. Entering via the main gate, we found a grid of narrow streets and alleys separating the various holding tanks, processing stations, warehouses, and storage lots that comprise such places. Junk and refuse everywhere, most of it moldering and rusty. The place was a ghost town. No telling how long since it was last operating, but the air still had that gas-station stench, like a coating that clung to every surface. It was also immediately clear that if anyone hopped the outer fence, they would have unlimited nooks and crannies to hide in. We had to make sure no unauthorized personnel got anywhere near our perimeter. That meant eyeballs on every avenue of approach and every inch of fence line twenty-four seven. Multiple daily patrols at staggered intervals in case anyone was trying to memorize our timetable.

Nothing on the site was supposed to be working, but we gradually became aware of a muffled but ongoing series of blasts of what sounded like an air horn. Turning a few corners, we came upon a windowless, two-story blockhouse that seemed to be the source of the sound. My subordinates and I exchanged curious glances.

"You figure that means something, sir?"

"Maybe they left the fridge open."

"It's like *Star Trek* when they go to battle stations."

The iron double doors were locked. Another door around back was locked as well. I had keys—at least sixty. Some labeled in Arabic, most not at all. I tried one at random, then four or five more. "I'm not sure this is really an issue, gentlemen. If something was going to blow, it probably would have happened weeks ago."

With a collective shrug, we moved on. Our mission was to hold the place until American engineers and plant managers arrived. Some were in the country already; we had escorted delegations of these grizzled Texas wildcatters to various sites. Most of them said they had never seen facilities in such a state. Here was a country that could have had everybody living on Easy Street, but that was not what Saddam wanted. His family, cronies, and a few favored clans made out like bandits, while twenty-three million other people got the scraps. I always thought oil men were a bunch of sharks, but the tool pushers we met seemed determined to set things right for a populace anyone could see had been long abused. We had brought freedom to the Iraqi people, but freedom tastes better with a few bucks in your pocket. Trouble was that there were not nearly enough experts willing and available to fly over. Iraq had a thousand facilities, all of which needed an upgrade. The best we could do was keep our corner unmolested until the provisional government figured out where we stood on the priority list.

We made camp within sight of the main gate, and I set up a patrol schedule. Thankfully, the surrounding area was likewise deserted industrial lots and storage depots, so anything that moved almost immediately came to our attention. Our first burst of excitement came that first night when a perimeter patrol reported possible intruders inside the wire via night vision. I immediately formed a squad to check it out. Once inside the gate, I split them into five pairs, sent them off in different directions, then headed for the "town square" with my radioman.

Whatever it was, or might have been, we found no trace of it. Best I can figure is wild dogs able to slip through small openings in the fence; we had noticed piles of hardened dog crap here and there. Even the wiliest enemy agent could not have obscured his own heat signature. We had probably scrambled for nothing, but guarding a place this big was a new ballgame. Our previous oil assignment was a pumping station in the foothills east of the city, a McDonald's-sized place, easy to watch.

I was about to stand down my recon when I heard those muffled building alarms again. We had ended up near that mystery command center, but I was not going to start fumbling around it in the dead of night.

My radioman looked to me. "Are you even a little bit concerned about that, sir?"

Well, yes. Warning systems do not just ring and ring for no reason. But curiosity, which eats at every bored guard, was one thing. Leadership meant deciding how far to take it.

It is also natural to get curious when you are standing guard because there is not much else to think about. But I had learned a hard lesson about that on our first assignment after the fighting. It was a roadside checkpoint near a small hamlet, and we were providing extra security. We had already been in firefights during the war, exchanging fire with enemy forces, but up to that point we had never come across the bodies of the men we had engaged. Guys from the unit we were supporting described seeing a dead Iraqi soldier lying in a culvert not far off, and the more mind-numbed we got from all the nothing happening, the more some of my guys wanted to check it out. I felt the same way. The war was over, and I had not seen even one battlefield casualty, which seemed like something people back home would expect a combat veteran to know about. So highly aware that we were reenacting the classic eighties flick *Stand by Me*, a few of us set off on a short hike to take a long, good look at our first dead body.

And, of course, the minute we saw it, we knew we should have left well enough alone. It was a guy about our age, ripped open, bloated, stinking, splayed unnaturally in the dirt. My reputation was not in the least improved for having seen it, nor could I ever erase the image, and I only went along because I was bored. Now I know there are things worse than boredom. So I walked away, reported the exact location of the body to headquarters, and continued my mission of guarding Iraq's oil.

Day 2: Another blip of excitement. This decrepit-looking big rig, belching smoke, gears grinding, pulled off the main road a half mile away, then came down the access road toward our place. We heard it way before we saw it, so I got up from the worktable I used as a command post and headed out to join the squad assigned the main gate.

We walked out a hundred yards to meet the thing in case it was militants trying to roll up with a truck bomb and started signaling to them. After repeated warnings in Arabic, and lots of pantomime, two guys finally climbed down from the cab. One middle-aged, the other a teenager, maybe the driver's son, their clothes and shaves about average for the Iraqi working class. With no interpreter, conversation was limited. They had come for something. We mimed no; they could not go in. It went back and forth, but the older man did not seem upset, and they were not armed, so we kept the tone firm but cool. I motioned them to open the truck's big back doors, and the driver finally did. He was hauling machinery of various types; maybe they were mechanics. In any event, we sent them on their way, and they slowly pulled their rig around and chugged back toward the main road. Five minutes after they were gone, I was kicking myself. We should have climbed in and checked their load more closely. They could have had stacks of artillery shells or crates full of grenades back there, and I just let them drive off. Guard duty leaves too much space for imagined possibilities, and as the leader I had to decide which of those possibilities mattered.

The whole thing was probably nothing, an innocent mix-up. But what if it was not?

Maybe it was a probe, some kind of test run, and I let them out to take a look around. Were they counting my soldiers, calculating how many of us were there, gauging our response? Maybe they would be back in force. This is what guard duty does. It gets your mind going on every possibility. What you did not know, what you did not plan for, all the clues you might have missed.

Like a frickin' alarm bell in a building you did not think was worth wasting time over.

I was responsible for every inch of the place. I should know everything about it I possibly could. Maybe that control center was locked because they did not want us in there. Maybe it was a weapons cache. Or components for weapons of mass destruction, the whole reason we were in Iraq. What if that building was some kind of Trojan Horse? Underground bunkers and tunnels crawling with Saddam loyalists, ready to burst out for a counterattack. None of which explained why an alarm was going off, but this known unknown was squeezing me like a migraine headache now.

I found a half squad of my off-duty guys in a circle playing hacky sack, told them what I was thinking. Fifteen minutes later, we geared up, and I opened the gate.

Approaching the control building, that alarm was still going, and all I wanted to do was make it stop. Started with the keys. First forty, zip. Forty left; if it was not here, I would blow the door with C4. As usual with such things, it was one of the last few keys I tried that finally did the job.

Pitch-black inside; swept it by flashlight. Some kind of admin area. Desks with ancient typewriters, adding machines, blackboards packed tight with fading numbers. Alarm louder inside, of course—bleating, insistent, scolding. We filtered in, weapons ready, footsteps sending up dust. No computers or electronic consoles. Heavy industrial doors around the room opened onto industrial hallways. I motioned us down the one the sound seemed to be coming from.

Off the hall were machine rooms, storage rooms, washrooms. Nothing active, nothing critical. Then stairs. Leading down. We had come in at ground level, so down meant underground, and that alarm only getting louder. Not earsplitting, but definitely nerve-racking. We came to another set of solid double doors. Whatever it was had to be on the other side.

They opened easily, into the kind of master control room you see in every action movie. Rows of consoles, banks of monitors, and dozens of red and yellow warning lights, all blinking in sync with that clanging, honking bell.

Was it some kind of pressure issue? I had seen something like that at the first substation we stopped to guard for just two days before getting another mission. When we pulled up, an Iraqi man covered in grease was standing over a large spigot that was pouring gasoline. A lot of gasoline. It did not pool around the open tap but went straight down into the ground, hundreds of gallons, enough to give any ecologist a heart attack. I asked the Special Forces officer we were relieving what the hell was going on. "He's an engineer. They stop by every few days to relieve the pressure." The man did not look like any engineer I had ever met, but he cranked the valve open and the fuel came gushing out.

Staring at the consoles now, I thought about the two Iraqis who had driven up to our gate in that smoking rig. Maybe they were not scavengers at all but the engineers meant to keep this place from cooking off. *Had I waved them away and left us sitting on a pressure bomb, alarms wailing because the system had no one to bleed it off?*

Looking over the various basement work stations, I realized it was futile. None of us had the slightest idea what any of these gauges or readouts meant. I was hoping we would find a wall-mounted Main Alarm Cancel button the size of a frisbee, but of course there was nothing. The migraine I had imagined before suddenly felt a lot more real, like a pinched nerve where my spine met my skull. I could feel my guys looking at me, as if to say, "Yeah, so, like, what now, sir?"

One of them seemed like he was kind of out of it. Private Watkins, monster-truck fanatic from Jacksonville, head down, rubbing his eyes.

"Watkins, you all right?"

"Yes, sir, no, just, like, a headache, sir."

"Same here. We need to kill that bell."

Private Carvel came to check on his buddy. When Watkins repeated about his headache, Carvel looked at me in surprise. "I got the same, sir. Sudden headache? Hurts like hell?"

I looked around the room. Only saw three other guys checking the tech, which meant somebody was missing. Redcrow, our hacky sack champ from Bluff, Utah. I trained my light around. A few seconds later, he emerged from a side room.

"Got anything, Redcrow?"

"Weirdest thing, sir. It's tables and chairs—only there's a bunch of dead birds there too."

"Dead birds?"

I do not know about my men, but what popped into my head was canaries in a coal mine. I knew the old story. Miners carried canaries in cages into the shafts because the birds were more sensitive to dangerous gases. If the canary stopped singing or died, the miners knew they only had a short window to get out before the air killed them too. That image hit me hard.

I think I went pale. Alarm bells? Headaches? Dead birds? We had walked into a death trap.

"Listen up, gentlemen! We are packing this in and heading out."

"Sir? I think this doohickey measures—"

"Leave it, Sergeant. I want everybody out of here ASAP! Let's move!"

They moved. I let them lead and brought up the rear in case anyone collapsed.

No one did. Not until we got back outside into the most beautiful daylight I had ever seen, where Private Billings started heaving. My head was swimming, and I figured I was about to join him.

I closed and locked the double doors, then we beat feet back to the main gate, reported to higher, and never went back inside the whole two weeks we were there. Nothing blew up, but I was not taking any more chances. I figured I would talk with the engineers about it when they showed up, but no one ever did. When our hitch ended, I handed off the keys to a younger lieutenant, told him what I knew about the alarm, and off we went. I never heard another word about that place and doubt I could even find it on a map now.

LESSON: BE CURIOUS

Something I learned in the military was to keep growing. Some think it is only about the physical growth of working out every day. That is for sure a huge part. Soldiering, infantry life, is about carrying heavy rucksacks, weapons, and ammo across long and hard distances. But being a soldier is also about mental growth. You study history, tactics, regulations, enemy forces, geography, culture, strategy, and more.

I took that growth to heart in my life. My motto became this: Learning is living. Being curious is one of the best ways to learn. Curiosity drives you to find new areas of knowledge, to dig deeper, to discover what others overlook. I still work on my physical and mental health every day, and I still try to learn something new every day.

In fact, constant curiosity, a constant thirst for knowledge, helped me land a job that changed my life. The way I consumed news, studied new areas like psychology, history, military science fiction, and technology, set me apart. While others listened to music during workouts, I devoured audiobooks. When I applied to join a think-tank–style group the top four-star general in the US Army was creating to do unconstrained advisory work, my approach to knowledge helped me get in. To my surprise, my mentor, the late David Johnson, noticed the way I pursued learning and recommended me. That curiosity earned me the job.

I am not sure where I first learned about canaries in coal mines, but I think it helped me and my men that day.

Be curious. Seek growth every day, both physical and mental.

It is a wonderful thing, but like the proverbial cat found out, you have to do it smart. In Iraq, I learned that curiosity can open doors you never should have touched. Sometimes it teaches you what you need to know. Other times it can kill you.

The art is knowing the difference.

Curiosity, my friends. The trick is knowing when to follow it and when to walk away.

CHAPTER 12

THE ROAD TO ECHO

WHEN MY BOY TURNED SIX, one of his birthday gifts was a Hot Wheels track. We set it up together, a simple father-son moment. The layout started with two parallel tracks hanging off a table. The cars whooshed down to the floor, where the two tracks crossed, then looped around to a floor plate with motorized rollers that spit the slowing racers on through the next lap. There's always a chance two cars released simultaneously will collide at the crossing. They'd hit with a sharp, metallic *smack* and go flying into the air. Predictably, that was my son's favorite part.

Smick! Smack!

He was rolling around the floor laughing.

Smick! Smack! Crack!

It started to wear on me. With only one "ambulance" for all those imaginary crashes, I tried the best ruse I could think of. "Hey, buddy. I think I hear the ice-cream man!"

Thankfully, he rolled to his feet and took off like a shot for the front door.

There is an old Army saying: No good deed goes unpunished. And I learned it the hard way in Iraq. My single worst experience in Iraq was the not-so "Silent Night" when I thought it would be nice to play Santa.

The good little boys who deserved presents were the platoon at Patrol Base Echo, a tiny outpost in the middle of nowhere perched on the imaginary line between our company's sector and the wild, wild West. Like most patrol bases, Echo was bare bones and stripped of comforts. No running water. No electricity except what the radios demanded. No food beyond daily deliveries or the dependable MREs.

Not that we were living in luxury thirty miles away at our COP on the former Tuz Air Base, but at least some makeshift Christmas trappings were sprouting. Strings of lights hung across doorways. Spirits lifted after Saddam's capture. Images of the bedraggled tyrant being rooted out of his spider hole had given everyone a jolt of optimism. Maybe the war had turned a corner. Maybe the fight was finally winding down. What did his loyalists have left to fight for?

Supplying Patrol Base Echo was my responsibility. Every few days we brought them a resupply of MREs, a hot meal, their mail, and whatever else we could cram into our limited trunk space. With the holiday cheer in the air, I was glad that on this trip we were carrying something special. Along with the hot food in insulated mermite pails, I had fresh apple and cherry pies to sweeten Echo's usual allotment of water and rations.

Like Santa, we moved under the cover of night, but instead of eight tiny reindeer, I had four Humvees. The drive was a straight shot south along the two-lane Route 2 that cut through the Big Empty from Kirkuk to Baghdad. For stealth after dark, we never drove with lights, navigating by night vision goggles. A few weeks earlier, our battalion commander had been critically wounded when insurgents ambushed his small convoy after spotting their headlights. We were not going to make the same mistake. Northbound traffic was sparse, just the occasional car or truck, some of them running dark like us. Our hour on the main road passed without incident; then we turned west, not far, and reached Echo's position, a small building ringed by mud walls. It had probably been built to house six or seven people, but now forty soldiers were crammed inside, thirty-nine grunts under the command of a single lieutenant.

Echo was glad to see us. Glad to see anybody, really, and between our two platoons, we made short work of the unloading. My counterpart, Lieutenant Fitzpatrick, was a cool-headed newbie by way of Virginia, and we took a stroll around the scrub to talk.

"How's the wasteland treating you?"

"It's like the ocean, John. The dust blows forward and the dust blows back."

"Think of the stories you'll tell. Fitzpatrick of Arabia."

"That'd be a pretty short movie."

"At least they won't be able to smell you. I should've brought some Irish Spring."

"I *like* being funky. My guys piss and moan to each other instead of coming to me."

We stood quietly for a minute. The stars so bright overhead, the whole galaxy on display.

"You need anything out here, brother? I mean, apart from everything?"

"We're good, John. Just don't forget about us."

I promised we would not. It was nearly midnight, time to head home.

I gathered my crews, we fired up our rides, and Lieutenant Fitzpatrick and I exchanged nods. Just as we began to roll, a call came from my fourth vehicle: engine trouble.

"Great," I muttered, and called a halt. The convoy came to a standstill.

Minutes passed. No update. I hopped out, strode back for a look.

The hood was up, three men studying the engine as Sergeant Martinez groped below the dash. "Could be the TSU, sir," he reported. "Or a burned-out relay or something in the glow plug control box, but I don't have the tools to get in there."

I searched the night sky. If repair was a no go, I couldn't tow it either, and there was no AAA in Iraq. We'd have to leave it out there until the Transpo guys back at the COP could send a contact team. Lieutenant Fitzpatrick was fine to car sit, so I directed my stranded crew to grab their gear and find a seat in another vehicle. At least this one could not be pinned on us. All four trucks were hard used and newly assigned to us. And after nine months in service here, anything mechanical was in serious need of a tune-up.

We set out again. Picked up Route 2 some minutes later and headed north.

In the black of the moonless night, we couldn't see lights anywhere ahead, behind, or in the surrounding countryside. It was like rolling through outer space. Which the bad guys could use to their advantage, so we had to stay frosty. But people were tired. My guys had largely fallen silent, no banter coming over the radio, so when Sergeant Dan Currie's voice broke in, it startled us. "Sir, I need to pull over."

I took the mic. "Talk to me."

"I think we just had a freakin' blowout!"

I rubbed my eyes. *What else could possibly go wrong tonight?* "Copy that. All vehicles, slow up, and let's pull it to the side, gentlemen."

I checked the digital map. With no obvious terrain features to sight off, I trusted what it said, which was that we were halfway home. Told my guys to sit tight, exited, and walked the ten meters back to Currie. He and Baltz were checking their front wheel well by flashlight. One look, and I saw he was right.

A dead tire. Unbelievable.

Kind of a nightmare too. Humvees have run-flat tires inside them, meaning that if a tire is shot out, you can still drive on it to get out of an ambush, but we still had fifteen miles to go. If we rolled slow, we would be out there all night and probably grind it down to the axle anyway. Nor could I just leave it this time. For security, US troops were not allowed to drive anywhere in Iraq with fewer than three vehicles. All I could do was radio the COP and wait for a repair crew. How long would that take? I checked my watch—0030 hours. Suppose some night-owl insurgents drove by and saw three parked Humvees. How fast could they arrange a pickup-truck strike force?

I made the call.

Transpo was understanding, giving me the standard line to sit tight because help was on the way.

We sat tight. Aside from the men manning the main guns, the rest of us got out and set up a standard security perimeter. Not that we could see much. Once in a while, distant headlights appeared. We'd watch the coming glowing cone for minutes until the Iraqi civilian vehicle passed, the drivers glancing curiously, but not too curious.

An hour dragged by. At one point a stray dog wandered across the road, the only movement we saw.

Seventy minutes. Eighty.

Finally, around 0215 hours, fresh headlights appeared on the northern horizon. Five minutes later, our saviors rolled up, thankfully under the direction of a senior warrant officer named Tompkins, a crew chief widely known for the care he took with both men and machines.

His boys got to it and had us ready to roll by 0245. When Mr. Tompkins asked if we needed anything else, I told him about the clunker left at Echo. He rubbed his chin a good while, then figured since we were halfway there, he ought to fix it tonight while he had the crew with him.

Sure, why not? I didn't need any sleep before my next day started at the crack of dawn.

I agreed to lead, and the two of us returned to our vehicles. I radioed my guys and explained the plan. I told my driver, Private May, to prepare to turn. He asked the gunner, PFC Brooks, if it was clear. From his higher vantage point, Brooks scanned with his night vision goggles as far as he could, gave the quick "clear" sign, and May began the U-turn with the rest set to follow. He put the Humvee in gear, wrenched the wheel, and we swung back toward the southbound lane. Before he could finish the turn, everyone heard what they later described as a sickening *smack!*—a million times louder than any of my son's future Hot Wheels crashes.

I didn't hear it because I was unconscious.

It felt like all I did was blink, but a lot had changed when I opened my eyes.

Flushed, wide-eyed faces lined my window, all kinds of yelling and background hubbub, and my body felt like I'd been hit by a truck. I brought my hand to my face, realized my helmet and glasses were gone and that I was covered in a debris of ammo cans, water bottles, and stuff from the inside of the vehicle. I adjusted my neck a fraction of an inch. It was sore but not broken, and then my driver came into my peripheral view. Private May was chalk white, trying to stay calm as his buddies at his window begged him to hang on, but I couldn't see what his problem was...until I glanced down. There was blood in his lap, and then I saw his door had been smashed inward and that jagged pieces of the metal interior had punctured his leg.

Something had hit us *really* hard. Was it an RPG? Roadside bomb? No, there was something else outside May's window. Wreckage of some other vehicle, but whose?

I craned my neck, found Sergeant Wood in the seat behind May in the same predicament. Pierced by shards, stuck in his seat. His door and window smashed too. Guys trying to help.

My door opened and hands pulled me out. Everything hurt like hell, but at least I could stand. I spotted Khalid, our interpreter, a few meters away. He had been sitting behind me and looked shaken but intact. Where was Brooks? I glanced up and back toward the turret, but he was no longer manning the heavy machine gun. Then I spotted him among the group helping May and Wood. I later learned he had been thrown from the vehicle, landing in a nearby field in a freak stroke of luck that kept him alive. The gun itself was gone, sheared off in the crash. But crash with what? Was it a suicide attack?

Nobody seemed to think so. It was an Iraqi civilian van heading for Kirkuk in the middle of the night without any lights on. It flew past our parked vehicles and T-boned us at what my guys all agreed was easily sixty miles per hour.

My blood ran cold. "How bad is it?"

"Trust me, sir. You don't want to see it."

He was right. Being in command, though, I didn't have much choice.

Still a bit dazed, I came around for a look. From the road, it looked like the van had slammed into a brick wall. The front was a splay of abstract metal sculpture, dripping with engine and bodily fluids. I had seen men torn apart in war, but nothing compared to the wreck in front of me. At least three corpses…or was it four?

"There's six, sir. It looks like those two in back are still breathing."

I saw that was true. But what I saw also made me think they wouldn't be breathing much longer.

Then I heard Wood cry out and turned to my own. "We need to call for medevac," I said.

"Done, sir. They're in the air."

Minutes later, the chopper was putting down, medical teams jumping out in full gear.

Minutes after that, more headlights from the north and what had to be every emergency rescue asset from the COP was pulling up in a semicircle around the accident.

I pulled my guys back to let the pros in. They had to cut May and Wood free, bandage them up before they could bleed out. Both were hefted onto litters to be whisked off by the chopper, but May wasn't having it. "I'm good, sir! We don't have to do this! Hey, Lieutenant?"

I came closer. The doc tending to him shook his head. "He's not going to walk this off."

"That bandage looks good, sir. That's all I need," May pleaded.

I knew where he was coming from—that soldier instinct to defy all adversity, to sacrifice, and to never leave your team or your family. Then I glanced at the wreck and at the dead civilians, now mercifully covered by ponchos. Should I have ordered the medics to leave May, to let him stay with us? No, they would have looked at me like I was out of my mind, so he was carried off to the medevac helicopter, yelling all the way. They put him on the chopper, which got him and Wood to the best Army hospitals, first in Baghdad and then in Europe. Following surgery and physical therapy, both were able to walk again, but not run, and both were discharged from the Army. May saw it clearly that night. Once he was on that chopper, he knew he would not finish the fight with his wartime family.

What May displayed in that moment was something I had read about in books, seen in movies about World War II and Vietnam, and witnessed many times already in our platoon in Iraq. Another aspect of a soldier's commitment to duty involves how they respond to injury. You might expect that being wounded is a golden ticket to get out of the war zone and return to safety at home. The reality is often the opposite. History is full of stories of soldiers putting aside their personal injuries or refusing treatment so they could stay with or get back to their small group, their unit, their family in the war zone. Many wanted nothing more than to ignore their wounds and remain beside their fellow soldiers, their friends.

As their copter took off, a second arrived. Every attempt was made to save the lives of the two Iraqis, but I heard later they both succumbed in the air. As all that was unfolding, I heard a calm voice behind me. "John?"

It was Captain Harris, my commanding officer, and I braced for a major ass chewing. My sole purpose in life was to keep as much crap off his plate as possible. And *never* wake him up.

He was definitely awake now. Surprisingly, though, he sounded more like a sitcom dad. "How are you holding up?"

"Good to go, sir. What I don't get is how any of us walked away from a hit like that."

"Must be the up-armor."

I shook my head in wonder. Five of my six assigned Humvees had no armor at all. The only one outfitted with actual armor (not the hillbilly attachments we slapped on ourselves) was the one they plowed into. Had it been any of the other five, everybody inside would have ended up just like those poor Iraqis. None of whom we were ever able to identify, by the way.

My entire right side was one massive purple-blue bruise. I rested most of that day when we got back to the COP, and by the next sunrise I was back on duty, patrolling in a new vehicle. The war was not over, and my duty was not done. They wanted me to get X-rayed, but I refused. There was too much to do, and all my parts seemed to be functioning.

Do I still think about that night after all these years?

Only every time I get in a car.

And in another year or so, my little boy will be old enough to get his learner's permit.

Maybe he should read this story first.

LESSON: DUTY

Duty is an obligation. As much as we should all serve something greater than ourselves, we also each have a duty. In the military, that duty is both moral and legal. The Army definition includes the simple but profound instruction: "Fulfill your obligations. Doing your duty means more than carrying out your assigned tasks. Duty means being able to accomplish tasks as part of a team. You fulfill your obligations as part of your unit every time you resist the temptation to take shortcuts that might undermine the integrity of the final product."

But duty is not only a military concept. It is part of everyday life. Every day we face temptations for shortcuts, temptations to look away, temptations to serve ourselves rather than others. To choose duty is to choose responsibility, to keep faith with those who rely on us.

That tragic night on the road to Echo revealed the many faces of duty. Supplying Echo was more than just another mission. It was our duty to deliver food, water, and mail to fellow soldiers living in hardship, and we were glad to do it. It was also the duty of friendship, of remembering not to forget those on the edge of the fight.

When the crash came, duty revealed itself again. It was in the soldiers who rushed to help the wounded. It was in May refusing evacuation and insisting he could stay in the fight, even when his body betrayed him. It was in the history of soldiers across wars who tried to push through their wounds to remain with their wartime family. And it was in my own decision the next morning to be battered and bruised but back on patrol because the war was not over and duty was not done.

The saying goes that no good deed goes unpunished. But that is not what happened on the road to Echo. That night was not punishment for a good deed. It was a reminder that duty is not measured in reward or punishment at all. Duty is measured in what we owe to one another, in what we choose to carry, and in our willingness to keep going when others are counting on us.

CHAPTER 13

THE ROAD TO SHUSHA

I AM NOT A HISTORIAN, but as an instructor and researcher at West Point, I spent a fair amount of time discussing "the classics"—the great historic battles that students, enthusiasts, and experts never seem to tire of. And the truth is that there are always more facts and layers of context one can absorb about Gettysburg.

The pivotal clash in America's most pivotal conflict, Gettysburg, is a compendium of strategies and tactics, and it also happens to be an immaculately curated historical site a mere five-hour bus ride from West Point. I've accompanied numerous faculty and cadet field trips there and debated the decisions of Robert E. Lee and George Meade with a hundred armchair generals. And while there's always something new to learn, Gettysburg is essentially settled history. A thousand scholars have pondered the view from Little Round Top in the last 160 years and written millions of highly informed pages about what occurred on those three days.

What a scholar truly craves is fresh material, an event not yet fully evaluated or classified by the graybeards. Galileo observing Venus. Marsh excavating the first brontosaurus. Jones's descent into the Well of Souls. Like those men of scholarship, daring, and action, I, too, loved the thrill and challenge of discovery. At the Modern War Institute, the center I helped build at West Point, we believe tomorrow's leaders must understand war as it is being fought today. There will always be a place for the lessons of Gettysburg and Hastings and Marathon, but military preparedness in the twenty-first century should balance the past with a focus on the here and now.

I fought in one of America's last major urban battles: the brutal street fight for Sadr City, the densely populated stronghold of Iraqi warlord Moqtada al-Sadr. That was nearly two decades ago, and the tools and tactics of war have changed dramatically since then. Today I study those changes at the institute, keeping my focus on the evolving character of modern conflict. I use every element of modern access to information, what we now call open-source intelligence. Civilian satellites, user-uploaded battlefield reports mapped in real time, social-media updates, and specialized journals written by and for defense professionals now offer a level of visibility that was unimaginable when I was on the ground.

In late 2020, numerous articles noted that new fighting had broken out in the disputed territory of Nagorno-Karabakh. That was news unlikely to garner attention from anyone without family in the region or some expertise in the former Soviet republics. Nagorno-Karabakh had long been a flash point between Armenians and Azerbaijanis going back to the early 1990s, around the time I first joined the Army.

Intrigued by this latest clash, I began watching for additional reports. Even with the world's attention fixed on the scourge of COVID-19 that year, social media made it possible to follow any conflict in real time. To my amazement, military leaders from both Armenia and Azerbaijan were posting updates and even responding to one another about where their forces were operating on the battlefield. I tracked every development I could find. Within a few weeks, it became clear the fighting had ended, and nearly all the territories held by Armenia for thirty years were back under Azerbaijani control. Ordinarily, that would have been the end of my interest. But one evening I happened to hit "Translate" on a Turkish news report, and I read how the tide had turned when Azerbaijani special forces scaled the sheer cliffs, rising more than four hundred feet, that protected the mountain city of Shusha.

Commandoes infiltrating and capturing an entire city? That was urban warfare. A decisive urban battle, and I wanted to know how they did it. It was not just news; it was a unique story of modern warfare. The kind the Modern War Institute was always looking for. I brought it to our director, Colonel Liam Collins—yes, that Liam Collins. By then I was retired from the Army and serving as chair of urban warfare studies, a full-time researcher at the very institute I had cofounded with Liam. He agreed it was worth a closer look. He told me to keep digging.

Easier said than done. Even before the pandemic, Western coverage of Azerbaijan was limited and reliable information even more so. I kept searching for updates on Shusha but found almost nothing. Months passed, life moved on, and one day I realized I still knew no more about the mountain assault than I had eight months earlier. Nearly every account of the war focused on drones, how they dominated the battlefield, changed the game, and supposedly revealed the future of warfare. I was skeptical. What about the fact that the decisive battle was fought in an urban environment, where fog had rolled in and nullified that very "game-changing" technology? What about the hundreds of soldiers who had to carry heavy loads across brutal mountain terrain? I had to learn more about the battle for Shusha.

So I brought Colonel Collins a new plan: We should go see the site ourselves. We had just returned from India the year before, where walking Mumbai's streets and speaking with people who had been there the night of the attack had given us insights no document ever could. He was intrigued but tied up with family commitments. I offered to go alone. Unsure but impressed by my boldness, Colonel Collins said, "Maybe. Keep working it."

We put out feelers to contacts in both Armenia and Azerbaijan, but all were rebuffed. Neither side wanted an American expert poking around. I was disappointed but prodded for any additional leads. Some weeks later, I got lucky. I'd been emailing with an English-speaking think tank director in Azerbaijan named Rusif, who now offered to host me for exactly the kind of research trip I'd been proposing.

Liam was torn. The war had been over for half a year, so I was unlikely to end up in harm's way, but the State Department was still advising against travel to the region. More than advising, actually. They had designated Nagorno-Karabakh a Level 4 "Do Not Travel" zone. According to the State Department, a Level 4 advisory "is the highest advisory level due to greater likelihood of life-threatening risks. During an emergency, the US government may have very limited ability to provide assistance. The Department of State advises that US citizens not travel to the country or leave as soon as it is safe to do so."

"So no one can go?" I asked him.

"No one associated with government. No."

"But I'm a civilian now. Does the Level 4 mean I can't go?"

"No, it means if you went, you would have to go as a private citizen, a blue passport, on your own. It is not a restriction. The government can tell its employees what to do, but ordinary people can fly wherever they want. Just remember: If you get in any trouble over there, you would be on your own. The Army does not officially know what you are doing."

"It is like *Mission: Impossible Nine and a Half*."

"Well, you are not spying, John. It is military research."

"OK, but what if something does go wrong?"

Liam and I talked it through. We came up with a plan that involved him using private resources to come get me if I ran into trouble. If there was anyone I wanted leading a rescue, it was Liam.

The key factor was that the war was over and my focus was on the recent past. I had no interest in challenging the status quo or taking sides about the region's future. With our rescue plan abstract but real, almost exactly a year after the end of hostilities, I flew to Baku, the capital of Azerbaijan. A modern, thriving, Muslim metropolis of two million, it offered every contemporary comfort imaginable.

The next morning when I climbed in the white van that came to pick me up, Rusif introduced two other men he'd invited along. One was a bureaucratic-looking Azerbaijani Army lieutenant colonel named Nihat, the other a bright-eyed journalist named Heydar. It was going to be a long drive from Baku to the area called Nagorno-Karabakh, even farther to reach the city of Shusha. Over six hours. As soon as we left the urban areas of Baku, I lost cell service. Rusif assured me there would be Wi-Fi at the hotel in Shusha, but I would be blind to track our movement on my phone's map and basically unconnected from anyone I knew while driving into the abyss. Great!

Heydar spoke excellent English and answered my questions about the territory and the types of forces involved in the recent clash. He had actually embedded with Azerbaijani forces during much of the war. Outside, the highway narrowed to two lanes as the suburbs gave way to crop fields and small villages, landscapes not much changed since the Russians seized this land from Persia, now Iran, in the early nineteenth century.

As we drove deeper into the countryside, a field appeared, marked by fence posts stretching as far as the eye could see. Barbed wire ran between them, and red skull signs warned of mines. For hundreds of miles the land was scarred by minefields, tank ditches, trenches, and old outposts. This was the former line of control, the divide between Azerbaijani territory and the land seized by Armenian forces during the first Nagorno-Karabakh war of the 1990s. At the time, it ranked among the most heavily mined regions on earth. The scene looked like a black-and-white photograph of No Man's Land from World War I.

Then Heydar pointed out an area with cities I had read about while following the war, places like Jabrayil and Fuzuli. But when he gestured out the window, there were no cities. Only foundations and a few broken cinder-block walls where thousands of homes once stood. Everything was gone. What I had followed in the news as key breakthroughs along the line of control were not cities at all. In many parts of the formerly occupied areas, towns had been abandoned when nearly a million Azerbaijanis were displaced, and they were never reinhabited or rebuilt. Instead, they had been dismantled by the Armenians, brick by brick. I had never seen anything like it in my life.

Heydar described the heavy artillery and tank battles it took to breach the line of control. Meanwhile, the army officer Nihat was saying something to Rusif, who spoke to the driver, who began to slow the vehicle. Glancing down the road, I saw we were coming up on an infantry squad moving west on foot. As we drew nearer, a few turned and waved for us to stop. Our driver obeyed, and I got my first close-up view of the victorious troops. Some were engaged in some activity on the road, but I couldn't tell what it was.

An older, grizzled sergeant approached the driver's window, not too pleased to find four city slickers crashing his party. He addressed the driver, but Rusif leaned over to answer, calmly but with authority, that we had all the necessary permissions to be there. Unimpressed, the sergeant studied each of us suspiciously. Then our colonel spoke up, even more authoritatively. And as they started to argue, I finally saw what that squad was doing.

They were sweeping the road with *mine detectors.*

My spider sense immediately started tingling.

The road west, the *only* road west, and they're looking for landmines on the very route Rusif was taking us? I'd learned a few lessons in the mined areas in Iraq. Like, *never* to walk or drive anywhere that might be booby-trapped with explosives until the engineers could check it out.

When Sergeant Grumpy finally seemed satisfied with our colonel's assurances, he motioned for us to drive on, around his men and farther west down the road. Then without warning, Rusif directed the driver to turn off the main road.

In my mind I was thinking, *Why are we turning off the main road?*

"Rusif, where are we going?" I asked.

"Just over there," he said. "Heydar wants to show you a bunker that caused the Azerbaijani troops a lot of trouble."

A few minutes later, we stopped and climbed out. Heydar immediately signaled. "John, do not step off the road. We lost a journalist here last week."

That got my attention. "You lost a journalist? What does this have to do with Shusha?"

"Just a few minutes," Heydar said.

I took my time. I did not step off the road and made sure to place my feet exactly where Heydar stepped. Another battlefield lesson reinforced.

We soon reached the bunker. Expended Soviet-style anti-tank and heavy machine-gun rounds were scattered everywhere. Rusif told me the story of two Armenian soldiers who had held the position for more than twenty-four hours, delaying the Azerbaijani advance. I appreciated the history, though my unease and frustration at the unnecessary risk were becoming harder to hide.

"Are we going to Shusha now?" I finally asked.

Rusif nodded. "Yes, no problem, professor. We go. We go to Shusha."

The colonel nodded as well. That was that.

Slowly, we eased back to the main road and around the minesweepers, some of whom looked no older than I had been when I first joined the Army—young men in service of their nation.

We continued on at a steady pace, with no other vehicles ahead or behind us. It was a beautiful day for a drive, but the farther we went, the more obvious it became that we were passing through a landscape of war. The countryside looked as if some giant hand had dragged across it, smearing everything in sight. Fields were scarred and broken. Leafless trees stood burned black against the horizon. It was a ghost region now, emptied of life.

The surrealism of the destroyed flatland was mesmerizing. There was almost a planned sequence in the churned-up ground, the twisted wire, the artful craters...and then, maybe a quarter mile away, I saw what looked like a small crashed airplane. Raising my binoculars, I saw it *was* a plane, but unless I was still daydreaming about World War I, the wreck appeared to be an old biplane of that very era. I looked again, then passed the glasses to Rusif, who asked the colonel about it. My question brought the man to life. He talked at length, hands mimicking flight paths and missile strikes. Heydar finally translated: "We flew those old relics in first to draw the Armenians' antiaircraft fire. The pilot would fly them toward

Armenian lines but parachute out of the plane right before crossing the border. The plane would fly into the enemy on autopilot. Then when the enemy positions revealed themselves by engaging the planes, we'd send in Turkish drones to destroy them. A good plan for us, yes?"

Biplanes and drones. The history of aviation in a single battle. It was also a textbook example of combat adaptation, the blending of old and new technologies. All war is asymmetric, each side trying to outthink the other, negate its strengths, and find an advantage. It would all be there in my future lesson plans.

More minutes passed before we finally cleared the wasteland and entered the forest, with the higher country coming into view beyond. The terrain shifted from flat plains and the scarred expanse of no man's land into steep, forested mountains. We continued to climb along an unimproved road that I later learned had once been a goat trail, widened by Azerbaijani forces as they fought their way toward Shusha. Heydar explained how the assault had divided into hundred-man companies that hiked for miles through the dense forest ahead to approach the fortress city undetected.

About an hour later, we reached a military checkpoint. The guards loitered beside the road as glum as that minesweeping sergeant. The soldiers checked my companions' papers without concern, but their eyes widened when they saw my American passport. The senior soldier eyed it suspiciously, then turned on his heel and disappeared into a small hut.

"Uh, hey," I ventured. "I'm going to get that back, right?"

The man ignored me. His soldiers stood around muttering, shuffling their feet, and drawing slowly on their cigarettes.

"I don't like this," I told my companions. I knew the risks of traveling alone, but losing the one thing that proved I was an American set off every alarm in my inner soldier.

They said nothing, and we just sat there, stewing.

I saw the senior man heading back to us. Unhappy before, no happier now. He thrust the document back to me and motioned our driver to move on.

Another hour later, a second checkpoint, and a nearly identical scene: My radioactive passport again disappeared into a field office, and tense moments again ensued before it was returned. This time the guard started lecturing us all about something. Pointing, gesturing.

"What's he saying?"

"We must not drive this road at night," Heydar translated. "Is too dangerous."

"Dangerous from what? I thought the fighting was over."

Heydar spoke with the colonel and then with Rusif and the driver before turning back to me. "They say there are still Armenian patrols out here. A squad was captured just last week. Twenty men."

I swallowed hard. Nagorno-Karabakh was not a former war zone; it was still an active one. That was why the mine detectors were out, why the wreckage still littered the landscape, and why every Azerbaijani soldier seemed to eye me with suspicion. If we had to obey an after-dark curfew, it meant I had already lost eight hours of field research time and had not yet seen anything. I began to take stock of what we had in the van. The colonel carried a pistol at his side. We had no long rifles. Not good. It was time to update Liam. I pulled out my phone and saw there was still no service.

"Not you worry, professor. Good Wi-Fi in hotel. Best hotel in Shusha!"

Yeah, that would be *great*. Assuming we got there before sunset. I desperately wanted Google Maps; another no go *sans* Wi-Fi.

"How far is it?"

Rusif pointed. "We start the mountain now, then Shusha."

I checked my watch—1430 hours. OK, we *might* reach Shusha before dark, but there was still plenty that could go sideways out here. I popped some gum, tried to relax.

"Another half hour," Rusif promised, and as I checked my watch for what felt like the thousandth time, Shusha finally came into view. Perched atop a cliff plateau, it was immediately clear why it had been chosen centuries ago for its natural impregnability. The only road up to it lay on the western side, the Armenian side, which made a surprise attack from these eastern woods an act of tactical brilliance. As we rounded the next bend, we came upon yet another army checkpoint.

Make that *two* checkpoints. One on each side of the road.

The first was run by the kind of Azerbaijani troops we'd already cleared. The second, I noted as we slowed and drew near, was manned by Russian soldiers. What were *they* doing here?

I recalled my research. Of course, the Russians were involved here. Territorial flare-ups like this were perfect opportunities for Moscow to entrench its influence and reassert power in former Soviet republics. Although Putin backed Armenia politically, he gave them no real support during the war and sent in his so-called peacekeepers only after the fighting ended.

There was no way to avoid the checkpoint. Thankfully, we were turning right toward the Azerbaijani checkpoint and Shusha and not left toward the mountain pass leading to Armenia, which the Russians were manning. The stop went much like the others, but this time I kept my eye on the Russians and let Rusif handle my passport and our paperwork.

Back on the road, as we circled the broad base of the mountains and began the main climb toward Shusha, I found myself reflecting on the realities of being a globetrotting military scholar. It was still exciting in its own way, but the thrill of walking into danger had long since faded after my tours in Iraq. I was a husband now and a father. I had a life beyond my career, one that would not be improved by ending up in a Russian prison cell. Liam and I had the right ideas—improving Army leadership through the study of contemporary warfare—but I had to measure risk differently now.

First, never go diddy bopping around sketchy places with people you barely know. Half the terror of today's ride came from wondering what other side trips Rusif and his pals might have planned.

As the van ascended, the view softened my self-reproach. It felt as though we were climbing up and out of all the scarred terrain, the battlefields below fading into quiet, green hills. This was what these countries had fought for, to breathe this air and see these views.

One final Azerbaijani checkpoint brought us into the city proper. Shusha had the look of a storybook citadel: stone walls with round towers, narrow walkways and arches, houses of carved stone separated by patches of grass. It was largely deserted, though not entirely. The new mayor was there to greet us, a cheerful, gregarious workaholic eager to show a distinguished American guest what his administration had achieved since "liberation."

Every Armenian family had left, taking only what they could carry, and the Azerbaijani families who would replace them had not yet arrived. The mayor was overseeing reconstruction, directing a fleet of cranes, bulldozers, and cement trucks as they worked to rebuild a city that had been left untouched for decades. The only other people we saw were army patrols. Armenian soldiers, the mayor said, still prowled the darkness. "It will be good," he added quietly.

The air hung with a yellow tint. Which seemed to have a peculiar odor. Was it...*fish?*

It was. Shusha was a ghost town that smelled like fish. Why would a city on top of a mountain smell like a coastal fishing outpost?

It seemed rude to ask, but I did anyway. The smell came from the Azerbaijani soldiers camped out in the abandoned buildings. Fish was a major staple of their rations. Despite the whole End of Times feeling in the air, I tried to stay on task. What was the full story of the Azerbaijani surprise attack?

Mr. Mayor was happy to walk us through it, and Heydar was just as eager to translate and add everything he knew. The whole place was a half-destroyed maze, but the mayor knew every exposed foundation, alleyway, church, and mosque and what actions had unfolded there. The elite troops who scaled the rugged mountains took the Armenians by full surprise. Breaking into squads, the invaders fought their way house by house, rooting out the defenders in a hundred bloody exchanges. Within hours, the Armenian leaders had fled, leaving the remaining troops as part of the spoils. Those who controlled Shusha, with its commanding heights and Olympus-like mystique, effectively controlled the disputed territories, so Nagorno-Karabakh was back in Azerbaijani hands. Mostly.

Far to the west, over Armenia, the sun was dropping below the horizon, and the mayor advised us it was time to check into the city's only operating hotel for the night.

It was little more than a guesthouse. Once more, I was ordered to surrender my passport at the front desk, which again chafed my nerves. But at least the establishment also boasted the city's only operating restaurant, with guests permitted to dine after curfew in an exquisite outdoor courtyard with breathtaking views of the surrounding country.

My fellow travelers and I sipped Turkish coffee, and the food was distinctly Azerbaijani: meat with yogurt, simple but rich. Given the uniqueness of the place, the long journey, and the tension of the day, it was probably the best meal I had ever eaten.

Had seeing this place been worth the time, effort, and trouble?

Absolutely. I couldn't wait to tell Liam all about it, and then I remembered they supposedly had great Wi-Fi here. Pulled my phone, got service, and hit our office number.

Liam picked up immediately and was much relieved to hear me in good spirits.

"Picture this," I said, unable to hide my enthusiasm. "We'll bring a dozen cadets out here. Do the mountain climb, just like the Azerbaijanis, then conduct land-nav and squad tactics about the ruins!"

"I love it," he assured me. "But I think we're probably going back to Gettysburg this year."

LESSON: DISCIPLINE

Many people think military discipline is simply about following orders. It is that, the "take that hill" moment when obedience and courage come together, but it is also much more. True discipline is doing the right thing even when no one is watching, when there is no order to follow. It is acting in accordance with your values and maintaining control of your thoughts and actions in the absence of supervision. Discipline is hard work, consistency, and goal setting. It is getting up every morning to exercise, not because you want to but because it is part of the job and because the job demands it. Like the Azerbaijani soldiers who climbed those mountains to reach Shusha, discipline is the endurance of both body and mind in the face of challenge.

One of the earliest lessons in discipline I ever learned came from my mentor, brother, and family, Leon. At Fort Polk, he showed me that discipline was the daily grind, the choice to put in the work when others would not. The military provides endless opportunities for advancement, physical development, specialized schools, competitions, education, and leadership, but only for those willing to outwork everyone else. Leon and I set goals and worked toward them every single day. We stayed late, studied, trained, and pursued mastery while others were content to simply show up and do their job. That was discipline—not waiting for orders but creating your own standards and living up to them.

It is not only the military that understands this. In every profession, from doctors and lawyers to investors and entrepreneurs, the pattern is the same. Success belongs to those who have the discipline to do the work every day without fail. The disciplined do not rely on luck or talent. They rely on habits and persistence. They do what others are not disciplined enough to do.

When I started writing, it was beyond hard. I did not know what I was doing, and I was not very good. But I had a goal, and discipline kept me at it, writing every day, learning structure, building style, and developing endurance for the work. Over time, I got better, faster, and more confident. The process itself was the proof of discipline.

Even going to Shusha was, in its own way, an act of discipline. It was dangerous and in hindsight probably too risky, but it was a commitment to do the work others were not willing to do. To go where others would not go. To walk the ground and gather the truth firsthand. That is what discipline gives you: the ability to act when others hesitate.

There is no secret formula, no shortcut, no magic. Nothing in my life or career was given. If you want something, anything, you must put in the work. Set the goal. Do the work. Excel. That is discipline.

CHAPTER 14

THE ROAD TO LAKE CHARLES

THERE IS ONE TRAIT OF the stereotypical image of the warrior-scholar I lack.

I don't drink.

People are surprised to hear that. It is so baked into the image. John Wayne tossing back a whiskey at the saloon. American GIs in Vietnam cracking a Budweiser. Vikings drinking mead out of ox horns.

I did try to drink when I first joined the military. I had no exposure to it as a child or teen. My mom worked three jobs and did not have time to drink if she wanted to. Well, maybe she could have, but it was not one of her coping mechanisms. She had enough anger in her nervous breakdowns to suffice. When I tried to drink, in some naive act of seeking acceptance, it did not go well.

"Ah," you surmise. "I bet John got totally hammered one night, something awful happened, he almost got killed, and that's why it's in this book." Or, rather, they look at my half ear today, hear that it was bitten off, and before I can explain, they all assume I was drunk in the fight.

Uh, no. I was not drinking that night or any night of great breakthrough to stop drinking.

I mean, yes, I almost got killed one night. And alcohol was a factor. And a motor vehicle. But it wasn't because I was drunk. "Oh," people say. And then they assume I'm a recovering alcoholic. A work-hard, play-hard type who played too hard, hit rock bottom, got into a program, and finally cleaned up his act.

No, no, no, and no. I am not an alcoholic counting my sober days.

First off, I was raised by a mom with her share of issues, but drinking wasn't one of them. There were kids in high school who drank, but that wasn't my crowd. I mean, I didn't have a crowd. I went to school. I came home. Regardless, drinking was not on my teen radar.

At seventeen, I joined the Army. At eighteen, I was in Panama.

Panama City was Party City. With three bars in particular that were known as places where underage American soldiers could get served. In that city, if you could reach the bar, you could drink.

My first Friday in the country, I listened intently as the platoon sergeant delivered our weekend safety briefing: "Those inclined to drink will exercise all due caution. Keep your tongues in check, and that goes for the rest of your body parts. The local ladies do not practice safe sex, and I guarantee fathering a bambino down here will bring a swift end to your military career. Same goes for drunk driving, drunk parking, drunk swimming, drunk boating, drunk hootin' and hollerin', and drunk roamin' the streets bare-ass naked. You get in a jam, you call me...only it better be a jam so heinous it's me or Superman you need."

It was the first of many such colorful briefings. Funny as hell the first time—not so much by the four hundredth, which is about how many Fridays I had in my eight years of soldiering before I was the one giving the briefings.

Did I exercise all due caution while drinking on the night in question?

Well, I didn't start any trouble. Spirits were high, conversation flowed, and I was putting away screwdrivers, which seemed the logical choice for a first timer. Nobody irritated me, and I didn't irritate anyone in return, until I vomited. All over the bar. And those around me. It's hard to remember what all actually went down, but I'd definitely gone in there with my buddies, and the next thing I knew, I was sitting on the curb outside. Alone. My head hung over my chest, and the new rugby shirt I got at the PX was soaked in regurgitated vodka and orange juice.

The passing señors and señoras gave me wide berth, but a homeless hombre in denim shorts and flip-flops took pity on me. He hailed a cab, helped me in, then climbed in after me. A worldlier young fellow, or a sober one, might have been alarmed, but my thoughts were awhirl. Thankfully, I was not shanghaied off to a sweatshop, nor did I have my organs harvested—just deposited back at the front gate of Fort Kobbe. I still don't know how I got from the front gate to our barracks and into my bed, but I woke the next morning with a splitting headache.

I resolved to drink more responsibly. Y'know, get buzzed, not wasted.

That's a fine line to walk when you're eighteen.

Eight months later, I was transferred to the 509th Airborne Infantry, based at Fort Polk, Louisiana. It was a dream job, serving as an OPFOR, a.k.a. Opposing Force, a.k.a. "the bad guys" in Army war games. Unfortunately, the one-traffic-light towns dotting the rural counties around the post were like graveyards after open-all-night Panama City. The nearest fun place was Lake Charles, a two-hour drive south. Week after week, our safety briefings warned us not to get plastered out there and drive back while impaired, and week after week, people did exactly that.

Fort Polk was also where I met Sergeant Leon Hall. I was a private, fresh from my first assignment in Panama. I had discipline. I followed orders. I did my job as instructed. Leon took one look at me and decided that just doing the job was not enough. He took me under his wing. He showed me what it meant to take ownership of your career, to build yourself rather than wait to be told what to do.

He made me run extra physical training every day. When the others went back to the barracks, we stayed on the field. He signed me up for military correspondence courses that earned promotion points. He talked to me about setting goals for every rank, every school, and every qualification I wanted. Even in the war games we played every month as the Opposing Force, he showed me how to lead and how to think.

In every army, there are soldiers who just show up to work, do their job, and go home. They secretly mocked Leon and then me as overperformers. But we kept pushing. We constantly tried to improve ourselves in every domain. Leon put that seed in me early, and I carried it through every phase of my life. Without that experience, without his mentorship, I would not have achieved half of what I did. He taught me that real discipline is not just following orders; it is making yourself better every day, even when no one is watching.

One Sunday morning I decided my drinking days were over.

I'd woken up fuzzy after another hard day's night. Hungover, I guess. I opened the barracks door, stepped outside, started to yawn, when a blast of pain hit my head—so intense it literally brought me to my knees.

It was my mouth. I brought my fingers up, prodded gingerly, and realized my two upper front teeth were mostly gone. It was the fresh air hitting exposed nerve endings that hobbled me.

When the dentist on post had a look, he figured I had tried to uncap a beer bottle. That didn't sound like me, but I wasn't going to argue with the man making the pain go away. Especially since I had no memory of what happened.

I didn't get proper caps for years. They just, like, cauterized the holes with cement. It was awful, but if you're considering quitting drinking, it's a reminder you never forget.

I weighed the good and bad of alcohol. The bad was stark: bodily injury, not to mention risking my career. Our platoon sergeants weren't kidding about DUI. What civilians don't understand about the military is we have our own justice system. A fancy lawyer can sweet-talk you out of serious charges in the real world, but the Army doesn't play. You mess up and you're out.

On top of that, I really didn't like the taste of beer or whiskey. If there's some trick serious alcoholics learn to make it go down smooth, I never did figure it out.

So what was good about booze?

Nothing I could think of. If my buddies called me a wimp, I knew they weren't my buddies, nor did I give a hoot about anybody else's off-duty expectations. I didn't like the taste. I didn't like the feeling in the moment, and I liked the after-feelings even less. But most of all, I was not trying to be accepted by anyone by following their behaviors. So that was it. I went dry and never looked back.

I still went out. I was a young dude who needed to unwind. Laugh, dance, see a pretty face. I just did it on Coca-Cola now. Sometimes I got razzed for it, but not a lot. And I soon found a new role for myself: designated driver. Those two-hour back-road rambles to and from Lake Charles were brutal, especially the return trips. People were thrilled to hand me their keys.

And before we helped each other survive Ranger School, my OPFOR squad leader at Fort Polk was Sergeant Leon Hall. Leon had a brother, Bob—country as a corncrib who was in the doghouse with his teenage baby mama—and Leon was going through a rough divorce as well. So when the two of them decided to commiserate over a bottle one night, I agreed to drive my two Miss Daisies.

I heard so much about the pitfalls of romance that evening I resolved to stay single, at least until the year 2000-never. Late in the evening, Bob Hall finally slammed his Coors bottle down and announced, "I got a buddy who can fix me up with ten months on an offshore oil rig. Ten months to get my head straight…and I'm takin' the baby with me!"

Leon and I tried to explain that wasn't the wisest choice, but Bob's mind was made up.

As we set off for home, we stopped to grab bags of Taco Bell. Bob started demanding we drive to his girlfriend's place in Natchitoches, two hours north of Fort Polk, so he could pick up the baby that night. When Leon argued he was in no condition to handle a young 'un, Bob broke down in tears. Luann was an unfit mother, he wailed. Out on the rig, in the company of good men, maybe his son could grow up decent!

By that time, Leon had nodded off, and I had to watch close the way the road curved this way and that through the dark woods, but I couldn't help puzzling over what Bob said. I mean, I'd never been on one of those platforms. Didn't they have lady workers too? Not covered in muck but doing payroll, typing letters and such? Maybe there was a daycare out there. Just think, all those rig babies, crawling around the floor—

The car was spinning.

The tires screamed, the headlights cutting wild, white arcs through the trees. The world became a blur of motion, blacktop, pine trunks, a flash of Leon's face, until one massive tree filled the windshield. Moss and bark rushed toward me like a wall. I hit the brakes, maybe too late, the smell of burning rubber filling the car, Bob yelling something incoherent in the back, then silence. We stopped inches from the trunk, the hood steaming, the engine ticking. The tree's branch hung in front of me like a finger of judgment.

Leon blinked at the bark pressed against the glass. "You fall asleep there, John?"

"Guess so." There was no further discussion. Later, in Ranger School, I'd learn how I could drift off at the drop of a hat. Standing up, squatting, prone; I was what they called a "sleepy Ranger." Useful in the field when you're dead on your feet—not so much as a cab driver. I put the car in gear, eased us back. Out of the rough, onto the shoulder, then the road, and on home without further mishap.

Almost killing my best friend was not something I took lightly, and that night remains the first and last time I ever drifted off behind the wheel. Thankfully, Leon didn't hold it against me. And after hearing the story, Bob was sure glad he couldn't remember it.

I still don't drink.

I owe that mostly to genetics and the gift of a nonaddictive personality…unless you're talking physical fitness, strength, and endurance training, which really became like a religion. I still work out today, but I'm more into quenching my endless thirst for knowledge. And in raising young daughters in the 2020s, I'm of course called to worship at the altar of Taylor Swift.

Can I give you a bracelet?

LESSON: BELONGING

Belonging is not the same as being accepted. Acceptance can be given to anyone, often without effort. Belonging has to be earned. It is the feeling that you have a place because you have proven yourself worthy of the group that holds it. In the military, in society, and in any team or family, real belonging comes from what you contribute, not from how loudly you demand to be seen.

Many people spend their lives chasing acceptance, trying to stand out, to be liked, to be noticed. They change how they talk, how they dress, or what they believe all to be accepted by others. But acceptance without substance is fragile. The first time you disagree or fall short, it disappears. Belonging is different. It is forged through shared effort, hardship, and values. When you belong, you do not have to announce it. You show up every day, do the work, and earn your place again and again.

That lesson found me early, and it began with Leon Hall. I had come to Fort Polk straight from Panama, a private who followed orders, kept his head down, and did what he was told. Leon showed me that was not enough. He taught me that just doing your job does not make you valuable. Making yourself better does. He showed me that you could belong to the Army, or you could belong to the profession of being a soldier. They were not the same thing.

He pushed me to work harder, to run extra miles, to train after others stopped, and to study when others went to bed. He signed me up for correspondence courses, made me think about what I wanted to achieve with each rank, each school, and each opportunity. He made me see that if you want to belong to something greater, you have to earn it every day through effort and excellence.

Even in our small unit, there were soldiers who only showed up to work. They laughed at the ones who pushed too hard. Leon and I were the overachievers they teased, but we knew the truth.

Belonging is not about being accepted by the comfortable crowd. It is about standing with those who live the values of the group you want to represent.

Belonging means living the values of the group you choose to stand with. It is not conformity. It is contribution. It is the difference between "accept me for who I am" and "trust me because I have earned it." A person of character does not chase approval. They uphold the standards that make belonging possible.

That is why I never had a problem saying no to drinking or to any other shortcut to false acceptance. I did not need it. I had already found where I belonged, in a brotherhood defined by service, discipline, and the quiet confidence of those who have proven themselves through action, not words.

Real belonging is not granted. It is lived, earned, and renewed every day.

DEFYING GRAVITY III

MY FAITH ISN'T THE KIND you'd notice on Sundays, but on sixty-five occasions I've prayed with everything in me. Not coincidentally, that's the number of times I've jumped out of perfectly good airplanes or helicopters.

Conditions and circumstances varied, but there's no such thing as a forgettable parachute jump. Each one is seared, crystal clear, in my memory. All Army paratroopers begin with five jumps during their basic course. Some of the people I met who never went on to join actual Airborne units still remember that course as the toughest three weeks of their lives. I never have the heart to tell them it was Disneyland compared to any jump they would have made afterward. Each one was a short prayer answered by gravity itself.

Happily, all my sky prayers were more or less heeded: sixty-five jumps, sixty-five landings without serious injury. That's what you pray for: *Please, please get me to the ground without major injury.* I always tell people I loved jumping out of planes; I just hated smashing into the ground after the jumping part.

That was the rhythm of it—jump, smash, repeat.

Oh, except that *tenth* time I went out the door. Little bit of a hassle there.

It was early in my career. Panama, to be exact, when I was basically a kid. Most US Army paratroopers jump once a month, but our unit made twenty jumps in only eight months. Part of that was proximity, as we essentially lived at the airfield.

Parachuting into Fort Kobbe was doubly unnerving because the base sits on a peninsula so small you actually exit the aircraft over the waters of Panama Bay and let the air currents guide your descent across the coastline to the landing zone. My first four jumps there went well, but as I'd eventually learn in combat, there is no threshold when parachuting becomes routine.

As you've likely seen on TV, squads of paratroopers emerge from their transport planes in rapid succession as their chutes bloom one by one. In reality, it's even faster, and there's a reason for that. The tactic of parachuting was tested and developed at scale for the US military in the 1940s, designed to get massive numbers of troops and their equipment onto the ground as quickly as possible. Everything about it reflects that purpose: the low altitude, the nonsteerable chute, and the short, violent ride that ends not with a graceful glide but a controlled crash. The parachute isn't built for gliding or sightseeing. It's built to drop soldiers, their weapons, and their gear straight down at the fastest speed still considered survivable. Supposedly safely. Most of them, anyway.

So when you go out that door, you're not only praying that your chute opens correctly but also that you're safely on your way down before the next soldier's boots come tearing through your canopy. Army parachuting is nothing like skydiving, where you have thousands of feet and several minutes to deal with any problem. Airborne trainees jump from about 1,200 feet, and in Panama we went out two hundred feet lower, which means the whole ride lasts about twenty seconds from chute open to impact.

On the day of my tenth jump, with a perfect tropical panorama spread out below, I stepped into the slipstream, that roaring wall of wind outside the plane, counted to four as I fell, and exhaled in relief when my chute snapped open. The opening shock always hits like a punch, but then, for a brief moment, you're floating. Everything slows, and the world looks calm. For those few seconds, it's beautiful.

Then I started to fall again. Which is *not* supposed to happen.

I glanced up and realized the next guy behind me was directly above and far too close. I made a snap guess what was happening—stolen air, because it is actually in the manual. There is a whole scientific explanation about aerodynamics and air pressure, but all you need to know is what I knew in that instant. His chute was disrupting the airflow around mine, collapsing my canopy and putting me on an express elevator back to Earth. Stolen air is just as dangerous for the guy on top. He started to drop past me, and suddenly our positions were reversed.

I processed all of this in about two seconds and was already halfway to the ground. If I did not break out of that bad air path fast, we would both be done. Instinct took over. I yanked the risers above my left shoulder, the thick straps that tied me to the chute lines. You cannot steer a big round chute like a small square one, but it is supposed to help. I jerked and jerked, the ground racing up at me, both of us yelling, "Slip away! Slip away!" The phrase is what you shout in any parachute emergency, whether it makes sense or not.

Then maybe a hundred feet from the ground, my canopy suddenly filled again. Before I could even celebrate, the planet hit me so hard and fast I did not have time to bring my feet together. Air punched out of my lungs. The jolt was like a lightning strike. For a second, everything went white and I saw stars.

At best, a paratrooper landing is like a regular person hopping off a ten-foot wall. You don't touch down like a ballerina and go skipping across the field; it's feet first and roll to your hips, and it usually hurts. In this case, I landed on my knees. And I didn't hit grass or sand or fertile soil—it was the gravel top of the unimproved road that ran down the middle of the drop zone. Pain exploded up and down my legs; I thought for sure I'd snapped something. After two or three seconds of lying in a fetal position trying to recover from the pain, some monster force wrenched me across the gravel and on down the road. This happens a lot: On landing, you need to immediately pop the clasps holding the lines to your harness, or your still-open chute can catch the wind and drag you off like a speeding car.

Hands scrambling, I finally pulled the releases and the dragging stopped. Silence fell except for the wind tugging at my chute. I lay there staring up at the blazing sun, watching giant silk flowers drift slowly toward the earth in perfect formation. My breath came in short, shallow bursts. Training kicked in. Time for the body check.

Ankles first. Always the ankles. I flexed both, waiting for the bolt of pain that never came. Good. Ankles worked. Knees next. A sharp sting, fabric torn, blood already soaking through, but the joints moved. No bones pushing through the skin. Shins? I pressed along each one with trembling fingers. Solid. No breaks, no jagged edges. I asked myself if anything hurt. The answer was yes—everything. My whole body was one long pulse of pain, but nothing screamed broken.

Relief came slowly, almost suspiciously. The knee that had taken the hit was already swelling, the fabric stretched tight over it. By evening, it would balloon to the size of a grapefruit. For the moment, though, I was alive, in one piece, and still on the right side of the dirt.

I figured I would just lie there until a medevac whisked me back to the States for surgery and a lifetime in a wheelchair. But after a while, my buddies came trotting up, faces ringed by the sun, looking down in concern. Their chutes still billowing behind them, they looked like guardian angels in combat boots.

"You OK?" one asked.

"Hooah," I grunted.

Hooah is the Army's universal word. It can mean yes, no, maybe, or go to hell, depending on tone. Bark it, sigh it, growl it—it always fits. Mine meant: *I'm fine. Don't make a big deal out of this.*

They helped me to my feet, then stepped back as I wobbled, grinning like an idiot, silently shouting to the world that I was still alive. I heard them muttering about calling an ambulance, which only made me more determined to move. I staggered over to my collapsed chute, reeled it in, rolled it tight, stuffed it in the bag, and started limping toward the rally point, every step pounding through my body like a jackhammer.

"Hey, you're livin' the life, Airborne," I kept telling myself.

Two weeks later, we were filing back into the C-27 for our next drop.

It was Number 11 for me.

Faith isn't just in God. It's in the gear, the training, and the will to get back up.

My knee still ached, but the fear was gone. The sky hadn't beaten me yet. And this time I knew exactly what I was praying for.

LESSON (FOR GRAVITY I, II, III): LIFE WILL HURT

Life will hurt. That may sound odd as a lesson, but it is one we all eventually learn. It will hurt physically at times and emotionally at others. If you live, if you try, if you put yourself out there, sooner or later you are going to get hit. And when you do, it will hurt. You may be knocked down. But you still get up.

The big, obvious wisdom in all of this is simple: Never get into a fight with gravity. It will always win. Gravity will pull you down every time, but it also reminds you that you are alive. Whether it is the first time you defy it by jumping out of a plane, the time you fall through life's chaos and somehow land on your feet, or the time you hit the ground so hard you are sure you will never walk again, the lesson is the same. Gravity always wins the fall, but you decide what happens after you hit.

In *Defying Gravity I*, I learned that fear and faith often share the same airspace. You cannot control the fall, only how you face it.

In *Defying Gravity II*, I learned that sometimes the weight of life itself can crush you, and that getting back up is not about pride; it is about purpose.

And in *Defying Gravity III*, I learned that even when gravity slams you into the earth, pain does not have to mean defeat. Every fall hurt. Every time I got up, I grew stronger.

Some criticize the saying, "Are you hurt, or are you injured?" They argue it teaches people to ignore pain and risk making things worse. But there is a difference between being hurt and being injured. Pain is part of life. Injury is when something breaks. Strength is not pretending pain does not exist. It is knowing what kind it is. It is being durable, unafraid of pain, but not reckless.

If someone is injured, physically, mentally, or emotionally, true strength means acknowledging it. Recognizing the wound. Not letting it define you but understanding that healing takes time, work, goals, and a plan. You do not grow by denying pain. You grow by moving through it.

The saying "no pain, no gain" is not just a gym phrase. In physical fitness, the goal is to create small tears in muscle fibers so they can heal stronger. Life works the same way. Some pains simply hurt.

Some injure. But many, if faced with honesty and persistence, lead to growth.

Do not fear getting hurt. If you get knocked down, make sure you are not injured, and then get back up, even if it hurts. That is how you grow. That is how you live. Life will always hurt, and gravity will always win the fall, but the strength to rise is yours alone.

CHAPTER 15

OPFOR RAMBO

THE CREEPIEST THING HAPPENED ON patrol one night.

Ten of us, two mortar crews, were moving through the Louisiana woods in the dark when something started following us. No moon, no wind, only the sound of footsteps that weren't ours.

Sergeant Hall halted us with a raised fist. The brush rustling fell silent as well.

We listened. And heard new movement: this time on the *other* side of us. No way that forest dweller had silently circled around us, which meant we had two shadows now, two unknown things fairly close at hand. Then the one to our left started *grunting*.

"Aw, man, what the hell is that?"

The city boys were confused. Us country boys were not. "Damn, Rodriguez. Ain't you never heard no pig before?"

"Pigs? Just runnin' around loose out here?"

"Shh!"

We kept still. Ears peeled. More grunting to our left. More brush rustling to our right.

Rodriguez snickered. "Here, piggy, piggy, piggy!"

"Zip it," Sergeant Hall hissed. "We're not on a farm. Those are wild boars."

Then we heard a *third* one. This time directly in front of us.

"What in the hell? They got us surrounded?"

Sergeant Hall wasn't laughing, and neither was I. We had wild pigs in Indiana. They shun human contact, but the last thing you want to do is walk up on one. There was a kid from our school who nearly lost his nuts when a tusk slit open his upper thigh.

The grunting grew more insistent. It was like they were talking to each other.

We clutched our weapons tighter, then realized they wouldn't really protect us. If it came to a fight, it would be primordial. Man versus beast.

The one ahead suddenly charged. We heard him coming, his grunts now a scream, and Sergeant Hall raised his weapon and fired a burst, which broke the still night. We were yelling, things were moving, foliage snapping, but nothing emerged, no flash of tusk, teeth, or hooves, and we fell silent again, frozen in action-figure poses...but whatever evil spirits our passing had awakened, no audible trace remained. We were alone again in the night.

People scoff when I tell this. "Ain't no pigs that hunt in packs," one woodsman chuckled.

But there were ten of us out there. We heard what we heard, and it wasn't some crazy dream.

What I know now is that it was a harbinger of our own doom. Because as dawn broke some hours later, our actual enemies hit us with a surprise attack that almost totally wiped us out.

We hadn't dug in, just assumed we were well concealed in an extra-dense swampy patch of forest. We took pride in our hide sites, places so miserable no one else would go. But somehow they found us. The first shots came from every direction, and my buddies were dropping before anyone could even organize a response. Sergeant Hall went down, madder than I'd ever seen him. Then Rodriquez and Dulan. Eckland, Tacoma, Ballou. The rest of us rolling around, trying to get eyes on a target, only we were past the point of defending a perimeter. Anybody still alive needed to be in fighting retreat. I grabbed for my rucksack, rifle, radio, a plugger—the Army's little GPS receiver—and hightailed it, tearing through the woods in the only direction I couldn't hear those telltale pops coming from.

Mad dashed for three solid minutes, a marathon in rough terrain, then took a knee for a listen. The shooting was over, just voices and victory whoops off behind me, but no one I could hear or see appeared to be in pursuit, so I granted myself another few precious seconds to think.

Had anyone else cleared the kill zone?

Hard to know from where I was. Maybe I could circle back. Take a look.

Gave myself another minute, let my pulse rate slow. A few cuts and scratches from tearing through the bushes and vines, but no serious damage. I was good to go. I didn't care to meet any strangers, so I made a wide loop back. Five stealthy minutes later, I could see what remained of our setup. Lots of the enemy standing around, so proud of their big, bad selves...*so* tempting to just pick one of 'em off. Hey, why not? I backed off a piece, chose a fallen pine for concealment. Took a good, supported firing position, my sweet time lining up my sights.

First shot—a clean kill! The guy was suddenly down, and none of his buddies knew what happened. They're looking, asking each other questions, but nobody thought of taking cover, so I took dead aim on a second guy and—*bang!*—took him out too.

More confusion. More milling about. Would you believe I picked off a *third* guy?

It's true. They heard my shots, but I guess they figured it was their own people, mopping up somewhere nearby. They really didn't get that somebody was shooting at *them*. But there was no other explanation for the little metal boxes on their shoulders now blinking and loudly ringing.

The Observer/Controllers confirmed it. "That's a hit, corporal. You're out of the game!"

Welcome to The Box.

A.k.a. the Army's Joint Readiness Training Center. Three hundred square miles of woods, marshes, and scrub in beautiful Fort Polk, Louisiana. Calling The Box a "game"—even a war game—makes it sound like fun. You think of paintball, laser tag, Civil War reenactments, or kids playing cops and robbers, but the Army has spent decades developing combat-simulation exercises that adhere as closely to real-world conditions as possible. And it all happens on some of the most inhospitable, rain-soaked, bug-ridden swampland on the North American continent.

Visiting units usually spend two weeks deployed into The Box for simulated war, and it is the longest two weeks of their lives. The Box is designed to be worse than an actual combat zone, and most veterans agree it is. But two weeks for us was Mickey Mouse. Our squad stayed in The Box for *ten months*.

That's because we weren't visiting. We were part of the show.

OPFOR stands for "opposing forces." A couple days before the next units arrive to train, we're already on the ground. Digging in, setting up, figuring out ways to kill them. The weapons are all real, but the ammo is not. Instead, every retort from an expended blank round activates a tiny directional laser beam from a little housing affixed to your rifle. If the beam hits one of the sensors strapped to every player's body, the sensor activates, and the instructors confirm your "death." That's the multiple integrated laser engagement system (MILES). So, yeah, it's basically Army laser tag.

Just because a kill shot won't break the skin doesn't make it less psychologically lethal. For soldiers dedicated to learning, training, and perfecting the combat arts, JRTC is the Big Game, and staying alive for two weeks is like scoring a touchdown at the Super Bowl. Not everyone makes it, but that institutional will to win, overcome hardship, and take out the enemy before he takes out you, burns fiercely in every pounding heart, every soul pushed to exhaustion. Also, getting killed in The Box doesn't get you a timeout. It means you're *out* out, i.e., you had your chance to excel, but the fates were not with you.

I knew for a fact that morning I had left three very unhappy guys cursing out their mystery sniper. The killings had stirred up a hornet's nest, and I had no idea how big the unit that hit us really was. A platoon? A company? From the number of voices yelling, I knew it was a lot. Sticking around any longer would have been pushing my luck, especially with daylight breaking, so I started trotting. I could hear my pursuers, but they did not have a vector on my location. I headed for parts of The Box that were not entirely unknown, a place where I could re-hunker, grab some chow, and figure out what I was supposed to do next.

Priority one: Get supplies.

I had my gear, enough to jury-rig a poncho shelter and stay warm at night, but without water and food I would not last long. There were still days to go in the exercise, and I had no clue what our superiors had planned. Maybe I could link up with another group and keep fighting with a new unit. We had done that before when only a few of us remained from a busted element. True, I had never done it alone, but it was worth thinking about. The pine grove where they had surprised us sat about two kilometers north of the winding ridgeline that overlooked the fake German village we called Busch Gardens, and Busch Gardens was the nearest supply cache. We had buried gear all over The Box, each cache holding food, water, ammo, and sundries for ten men, so if I could reach that ridge, I would not worry about the essentials.

Hiking to that ridge on my own was a whole new adventure. In a patrol, every soldier covers his particular sector. Alone, the danger zone is literally 360. I needed eyes in the back of my head and an extra set of ears. No further enemy contact, but the initial thrill of my miracle escape and badass counterattack had dissipated. Ten to one, the controllers had ruled us No Longer a Threat to the trainees and expected me to come in. JRTC is for squad, platoon, and even battalion-level operations; nobody is supposed to be roaming The Box alone, so they were probably mad at me already. On the other hand, wasn't the whole point of OPFOR to jam as many wrenches as possible into the trainees' plans? They wouldn't allow a lone-wolf sniper to run loose in their area in an actual war, so why should I make it easy on them here? Those boys came to play. All right, suckers. Let's play.

I got within a hundred meters of the Busch Gardens cache point, took cover, and scanned every inch of the surrounding woods for a good fifteen minutes to make sure no one was lying in wait. Everyone in our squad carried a list of our cache points. Suppose our opponents found them and radioed their buddies to close in? It was crazy, but no crazier than a squad of newbies getting the jump on us out of nowhere. They weren't Rangers or Special Forces, either, just regular grunts from the 101st Airborne. They must have gotten lucky somehow with intel. Had someone caught a distant glimpse of us and calculated our position? My unit had "fought" in dozens of exercises, and no one had ever turned the tables on us like that before.

When I was convinced there was no ambush or activity around the site, I moved to our hidey-hole just beyond a rock shelf and went to work clearing the thin cover of topsoil with my E-tool. When the bounty was revealed, I had this *Home Alone* moment when I realized it was entirely mine. I could open every MRE pack and grab all the chocolate-chip pound cake I wanted! But I was disciplined. I only ate three. It seemed like a just reward for all my derring-do.

After my luxury breakfast, it was time to get to work.

Among my gear was a PRC-77 radio, one of those bulky steel boxes from the Vietnam days, and I figured I should at least try to reach higher headquarters. Sergeant Hall usually handled our daily check-ins with command, but he had made sure every one of us knew how to do it. I had the frequencies for higher, but no idea who might be in range, since I had moved out of our area, or if they were even still alive in the game. I went through every channel, repeating the standard call signs, but got nothing but static at every turn. *Home Alone*, indeed. I switched off the radio and figured I would try again when I moved to a safe hiding spot.

For a second I had doubts. Now what? Do I hit the road, flag down anyone I see, and tell them I need to go in? It crossed my mind. I could quit, call it done, and be back at the barracks eating a hot meal before dark. Then the other voice cut in. "You best squelch that," I warned myself. "When the mind goes defeatist, you are done." I took a slow breath, packed up what I needed, reburied what I did not, and got moving.

As I hiked, I forced myself to think like we were taught in OPFOR. When in doubt, attack. We were taught to constantly adapt, not like some lost soul in the wilderness but as fighters who make a plan and strike. Take stock of what you have. Collect data. Outline a plan. Formulate the next attack on the enemy in your neighborhood. Short-term goals keep the panic down and the brain from running wild. You are alone, but you are still in the fight.

Once I set my mind to it, my job became attacking every unwary trainee I could find. I had the home-court advantage. We knew which parts of The Box practically begged for patrol bases and which roads every unit had to use to get there. The plan was simple. Hit fast, disappear faster. An old OPFOR trick was to leave something tempting in the middle of a road when you knew a vehicle was coming. A box of MREs, a poncho liner, a blanket—something that looked like it had fallen off a supply truck. Weary travelers would stop, step out, and reach for the prize. *Bang!* They were dead. It worked more often than it should have. The road attacks slowed communication between units, sowed confusion, and reminded everyone that The Box was never safe, not even on the roads that looked friendly.

I could pull this off a few times, if I was lucky. Once word got out, they would not be complacent anymore. They would start sending heavier forces into areas they now thought risky. Once the foxhunt began, my options would dwindle fast. I had skills, but I was not Rambo. Nobody ever is.

The most predictable campsite in the whole Box was barely a klick from the main entry gate, a picnic-ready plateau with land sloping down on three sides to the far-mushier turf below. We'd conduct a few long-range patrols around it, but usually dug in and waited for the enemy to come to us. The farther soldiers get from "home," the more mistakes they make.

With me, they probably figured I'd try to keep way out ahead of them. Popping up at the front door would be the last thing they'd expect.

Hiking a direct azimuth would have gotten me there in about two hours, but there was no way I would cross open country with the sun up. I stuck to the heavier brush instead, using the road as a handrail so I was never unsure of where I was, and hoped to make it in four. What I had not figured on was how much solitude messes with your radar. Everything means more when you are alone. Every bird caw and animal chitter, every strange odor coming off a bog, even the way the wind moves through the trees. Now I know how the rabbit feels when it leaves its burrow to forage while half its neighbors see it as a meal. I became hyperaware of myself too—the busted fastener on my helmet chin strap, boots that were not as waterproof as they used to be, the half roll of toilet paper I had left behind. All small things that suddenly felt like big weaknesses to a man with no backup.

I pressed on. Only the more I humped—up, down, sideways, under, through, and across—the more I was convinced all I'd find were obstacles in my way. So it was total vindication when at last the plateau came into my far view. The perfect ambush site. Now the trick was to infiltrate to within laser range without being seen by any passerby convoys. I had to get to the road to put out the decoy empty MRE box I had been carrying, then back up to my sniper perch.

There was higher ground that would have afforded better sight lines, but the best way to stay invisible was to find a little nest as close to the surrounding lowland muck without actually getting wet. I went extra slow, tree by tree, and finally found a fold in the land with enough brush for cover. Settled in to study my target options and mentally mark my escape route. By the time they figured out it was incoming fire, not a faulty sensor, I intended to be half a klick away.

I was set. A half hour passed by. The Louisiana sun blaring. There is a saying about combat (even simulated combat), that it is long periods of boredom punctuated by moments of sheer terror. I was in the long period of boredom. Hours went by. Waiting. Waiting. And then...dust in the distance...a lone HMMWV. Would they take the bait? Brake lights! Yes! An excited soldier jumped out to claim his prize. Steady bead. *Bang!* Ringing from the sensor on his shoulder.

I didn't wait to see any more. I took off back through the trees the same way I came and didn't stop until I was out of breath and drenched in sweat. My face was burning hot, and half of it itched like crazy. I kept rubbing and scratching, trying to figure out what was wrong, until I remembered the reason everyone in The Box ends up itching like mad.

Poison ivy.

That night I found a hide spot and took stock. My face was on fire. I knew now it was definitely poison ivy. The stuff grew everywhere. Fort Polk could have sold it as a cash crop. I hadn't been grabbing at any plants, but I'd had the rash before. Maybe I'd scratched near my eye and brushed against a poison oak or sumac branch. Sometimes that was all it took. All the rubbing, running, and sweating only helped it spread. I dug out my clean T-shirt and the half-full sampler tube of Cortisone, blotted the sweat from my face, and dabbed the goo on the worst spots. The rash was now crawling across the back of my right hand too, the one I'd been scratching with. It wasn't a miracle cure, but I hoped it would keep things from getting worse.

Once I settled into my hide site, the negative thoughts crept in. I knew the poison ivy would spread. Having it on my face was already bad, but I'd had enough run-ins to know where it could go from here. Hands and legs were tolerable. Throat, eyes, or groin meant a full-blown emergency and a steroid shot.

The negative thoughts kept circling. I was alone, miserable, and itching worse by the hour. Should I quit?

But I wasn't alone.

Back in the rear, command was growing frantic. They had an unaccounted-for soldier. To be clear, it is not normal to have anyone roaming the training area alone. Some of the higher-ups wanted to halt the exercise and send out a rescue team. But one man stood in their way: Sergeant Hall! He planted himself in the command center and went to war for me. From the deaths after our ambush to the mysterious road attacks, he assured them, "That's him. He's still in the fight." He held firm that I was alive, doing exactly what I had been trained to do, and that stopping the exercise would be the same kind of overreach the Army had been trying to fix since Vietnam. Sergeant Hall's word carried weight. Everyone respected him as one of the best NCOs in the unit, and he basically shamed The Box bosses into letting me stay out there on my own. The command stood down the search party.

By the next morning, half my forearm was bubbled and oozing, blisters forming between my fingers. It felt like someone had strapped a fire mask beneath my eyes. I was sore as hell from barely sleeping on a razor-thin plastic poncho when I suddenly heard voices.

I was wedged into a narrow cleft of rock. Anyone within ten meters would spot me. All I could do was lie there and pray that if they found me, they had more Cortisone.

I tried to gauge how close they were, what they were saying. They didn't sound like trainees, more like a couple guys shooting the breeze.

I finally dared a peek and put eyes on my guests: two observer/controllers sipping coffee. Exactly the guys I needed to escort me out of hell. The past twenty-four hours had been very real, but now I was just a pool of misery with nothing left to prove. These two could walk me out and save me the indignity of getting lit up by some trainee.

All I had to do was sit up and announce myself...but I couldn't. This was my lowest point in The Box, but I had never been a quitter. These exercises ended in victory or death, and a little discomfort on my part, or even a lot, did not qualify as death. Through my field mirror I could see the ivy rash was still below my eyes. It burned and itched, but it was not pain. And there were still trainees to be waxed. I fully intended to keep playing the OPFOR Angel of Death until higher headquarters explicitly told me otherwise.

So I stayed still. Even picked up some useful intel while the refs joked about the status of the aviation assembly area nearby. I knew that area. It was one we regularly attacked. Not more than a klick away.

Say no more. Within two hours, I was perched above the assembly area.

Taking a prone firing stance, I drew practice beads on the silhouettes moving below, two hundred meters off. Not an impossible shot, but no sure thing either. I keyed in on one figure who had to be a senior sergeant, just by the way he stood planted, fists on hips, barking orders at unseen subordinates. He liked to peer off into the distance, standing perfectly still, like he was General Patton or somebody. In other words, begging to get shot.

I waited until I saw an observer/controller loitering about ten meters from him, then fired. The shot cracked through the air, and sure enough, Patton's sensor lit up. He turned, yelling at his men, assuming it was friendly fire, but the ref was right there to set him straight. And just like that, I was gone again, hunting for my next sniper perch.

Following his successful elimination of the enemy's command vehicle, including three soldiers ruled "killed in the blast," Private Spencer was never seen again and passed that day into the annals of JRTC OPFOR legend. Some scholars believe he migrated south, down through Mexico to the coca countries, where he still wages a one-man crusade against the armies of the narco-barons. In the more mythic versions, he joined that pack of wild boars. In time, he became their alpha, and all the wild things in The Box still worship him as a god.

The real ending is less poetic.

I am still proud of my penultimate score. After knocking out a few more at the aviation assembly area and pulling off another roadside ambush, I survived another day and a half. Three days total, on my own and out of touch with higher headquarters. Like a phantom, like Rambo, I moved unseen and struck without mercy.

By the morning of Day 3, I was getting a little too cowboy for my own good. Instead of sniping at distant patrols, which gave me a better chance to escape in the confusion, I decided to creep right up to the perimeter of the assembly area.

The creeping part went flawlessly. I came up totally unseen behind an unsuspecting trainee sentry, only for my weapon to fail. The rifle went click but did not fire. The startled kid spun around and zapped me square in the chest.

"Say goodnight, Gracie," one of the two hovering observers declared. I think they were the same guys I had eavesdropped on.

While I basked in the mix of awe and disgust my poison-ivy-covered, unwashed body inspired, I knew I was finally mission complete. Once I had checked out medically, I reunited with my "dead" buddies and learned what a stir my three rogue days had caused back at Headquarters. Nobody had ever seen anything like it, and in the end, I walked away with the Army Achievement Medal.

After all these stories I've told you of me nearly getting killed, here it finally happened. And in this case, I have to admit, death felt pretty good.

A couple days later, well rested, well-fed, and rash free after a steroid shot, we packed up, left The Box, and headed home. Two weeks later, the game began all over again. That's the truth of The Box: You think you're alone until you remember who made you strong enough to survive it.

LESSON: NEVER ALONE

In the military, part of our creed is to never leave a fallen comrade. There is comfort in that promise, whether you are a soldier in the field, a nurse in a hospital ward, a teacher in a classroom, or anyone who has ever feared being alone. It is the assurance that your people, your team, or your community will come for you.

But even beyond that code lies a deeper truth: You are never truly alone. Even when you are physically by yourself, you carry the pack with you. The training, the names of the people who shaped you, the rhythm of their footsteps, the mission you share, and the look on a mentor's face when they refused to give up on you are all forms of company. They march with you in memory and in muscle. Every skill you have mastered, every voice that guided you, is still there in the silence.

In the field, and in life, you learn what every animal knows: the power of the pack. Even Rambo had a pack. No one survives on their own forever. A lone runner is quick but vulnerable. The pack gives purpose, mission, and belonging.

You may find yourself alone in a hospital room, an office, a city apartment, or a stretch of swamp, but you are still part of something greater. You move, work, and endure for those who helped you become who you are. That family lives in your instincts and reflexes. When the night is darkest, when your phone is silent and your doubts are loud, remember the ones who already stood for you. They are your rear guard, your conscience, and your proof that you are never abandoned.

Real strength comes from knowing that even in solitude you remain connected to others through shared purpose, identity, and memory. That truth carries beyond the battlefield. Today we live in a world of digital tribes and social networks, more connected than ever yet lonelier than before. A screen can link us instantly, but it cannot replace the bond of trust earned through shared struggle and service. Whether in uniform or out, online or in life, the answer to loneliness is commitment to others, the willingness to be part of something larger than yourself. You are never alone if you keep giving, keep belonging, and keep faith with your pack in war, in life, and in the quiet moments in between.

CHAPTER 16

ACE OF SPADES

GROWING UP, I HAD ZERO interest in becoming a cop.

Always driving around, parked somewhere, watching traffic, or hassling kids at the Dairy Queen who weren't even doing anything. We had a few around my town, but the one everybody knew was Deputy Bell. Reedy-looking dude, always working a toothpick, eyes that bulged out when he got steamed, always listening to what was going on, wherever he happened to be.

Me? I wanted *action*. That's why I joined the Army. Why I drove myself to be the best.

The minute major combat operations ended in Iraq in 2003, every high-speed soldier became something we had never trained to be: cops.

Upholding the peace. Maintaining order, such as it was.

There was also the matter of the fifty-two Most Wanted senior leaders of the old regime, which some Pentagon genius had the idea to print up as decks of playing cards and distribute to every unit. Some had color thumbnails of the outlaws, others just their names, titles, and a silhouette. Finding these guys was the ultimate game of Needle in the Haystack, even assuming they hadn't jumped the border. Sometimes word came down that one of them might be in our sector, in or around the northern city of Kirkuk, so I'd load up my platoon, forty men in eight Humvees, and go beat the bushes.

At least a manhunt was a clearly defined task. What was harder were all the days and nights we spent just driving from village to village. My CO preferred the term "intelligence gathering" to "presence patrol," but the upshot was that we were cops keeping our eyes peeled for trouble—for any sign of militant activity that might jeopardize the sudden, fragile peace.

We quickly realized one key to policing is being on good terms with the local populace. Which we didn't exactly enjoy. There was only one interpreter assigned to our company, and his place was beside the captain, who might be accompanying our platoon on any given day, but usually not. Which left me attempting to engage with the Iraqis largely by tone and pantomime.

The Kirkuk region was ethnically diverse, including Kurds, Shiites, and Turkmen who greeted us with smiles or offered us cigarettes. But there were plenty of pro-Saddam holdouts as well. These people glared when we rumbled past in our monster-looking trucks. Some openly cursed us, stomped their feet, turned their backs, or spit in the dirt. Most of the people we thought we had saved were unreadable. They looked down or away if you spoke to them. That is how you survive under a dictatorship. Don't say nothin' to nobody and ain't seen nothin' neither.

Now that I was a sheriff, I thought more about Deputy Bell. He had it easier, I realized. He *knew* Richmond, Indiana, because he was a local. Knew the hangouts and all the good hiding spots because he'd been a punk kid himself. When something went down, nine times out of ten he already knew who did it and where to find them. He knew because he listened to everything people said and filed it away for later use. His whole low-speed hick thing was just an act.

Well, I sure could have used him now. I mean, the Iraqi version of him. We were on patrol around Hawija, a notoriously pro-Saddam urban area west of Kirkuk with a terrible reputation. It was April or early May, and we still didn't have a fixed patrol base. When our shift ended, we pulled the vehicles off whatever road we were on, set up a perimeter, and bedded down in any abandoned government building with a wall around it, or even an open field. Which brought back memories of living out of the car as a kid... homeless, or just house-less, that week or so between my uncle's attic and my recently deceased grandfather's house. Maybe that was one more reason I ran off to join the circus.

Anyway, just as I was getting cozy one night in Kirkuk, some hot new intel came over the wire: a possible location for the Ace of Spades.

Jaws dropped. We couldn't pronounce half the names on the Most Wanted cards, but everyone knew the Ace of Spades.

El Jefe. Boss of all bosses. Saddam blankety-blank Hussein! About 168,000 square miles of Iraq to hide in and someone thought the fallen tyrant was *here*, in our sector?

Visions of glory flashed through my head. Conspicuous gallantry, headlines, ticker-tape parades, even a ridiculous image of a White House reception and the Bush twins. The thought came and went in an instant. This was beyond a serious moment. This was the mission of all missions, and unlike a well-planned raid, we did not have months to build a mock site and rehearse every detail the way they would for the bin Laden operation years later. We had minutes.

First things first. I called my squad leaders in and laid out what little intel we had: a suspected safe house west of the city center—a farm near the Tigris lowlands, not a fortified compound. Expect bodyguards and a fight. Reports mentioned suicide vests. Move fast but think smart. Keep your heads. Twenty minutes later, we were back on the road.

It would have been safer to skirt the town, but we didn't have time. Eight vehicles draw attention, so we rolled like any routine patrol. Many Iraqis slept on their flat roofs to beat the heat, televisions casting blue glows as we passed. We watched for cell phones, for anyone signaling ahead. The streets thinned into trees and scattered houses before dipping toward a smaller town center half a mile below. Our coordinates were just east of it.

We found the turnoff. I halted the convoy a quarter mile out and dispersed half the platoon to establish an outer cordon. They fanned out and disappeared into the dark. When the cordon called ready, I climbed back into my Humvee. Three vehicles tucked in behind as we accelerated the final stretch for maximum surprise.

The compound was nothing remarkable. Run-down, single-story stone longhouses, a low wall, a courtyard with a leaning date palm. It looked deserted, as if that were the point. I hand signaled Third Squad to set a tighter inner cordon. Then First Squad stacked up at the entry—short, crisp movements. I waited behind the wall with my radio operator. No one had time to fumble.

We did the basics the way we had many times before. A four-man stack to the door, weapons tight, eyes forward, index fingers soft on triggers until called. Breach on the squad leader's count. No time for a shaped charge or a multiteam demo. The door yielded with a boot and a shove. Flashlight cones cut through the dark interior like knives. The smell hit first, stale cooking oil, tobacco, and the sweetness of rotting fruit from a neglected bowl. A rooster screamed somewhere. People in the room froze in a way that told you more than any confession ever could.

Clearing a house that might hold a deposed dictator is an exercise in humility and speed. Room by room the squad swept. Weapons covered corners, muzzles down during the first quick checks, then up when the shape of an empty bed or the shadow of a closet suggested hiding. We found a middle-aged farmer and his wife in one room, eyes huge, hands clamped together like they were trying to stop their own hearts. Their fear was raw and real. Were they terrified for themselves or for a guest they could not admit to harboring? No guards, no weapons on their persons, nothing behind the curtains but the slow flicker of a cheap television.

Without an interpreter I could not triangulate their answers, so we did the other thing we always did. We secured and we searched. We turned every mattress, opened every pot, checked every crawlspace, crawled through attics, scraped straw aside in the barn. Men worked with methodical force. Some of the men joked quietly about the headlines we might get. The jokes were thinnest when we found nothing.

There was the constant, quiet terror of assuming the worst. Reports of suicide vests meant every tucked bundle of clothing could be a lethal device. We moved with a mixture of haste and reverence for that possibility. I had a guy check belts and backpacks. Another layered a blanket over a suspicious bundle and carried it out with the muzzle pointed away. Each small procedure was meant to deny the enemy the chance to surprise us.

After a full sweep and two hours of searching every conceivable hiding place, I had to make a call. We had no authority to blow the place apart on a hunch. We had civilians who were clearly shocked and broken by the intrusion. We had no positive ID and no actionable proof. I sat them at the kitchen table, hands trembling but compliant, and we did the things we always did when we had to leave with nothing. I mimed an apology and pressed a hundred dollars into the farmer's trembling hands. Standard compensation for splintered doors and broken sleep. We rolled out empty-handed.

Back on the main road, I keyed the radio. Stay alert. If they knew our route in, they could be waiting for us on the way out. I warned the driver we would thread different streets back through the town and keep our eyes peeled. We climbed the hill with lights on and nothing else stirring on the road.

US intelligence kept saying Saddam was still in country, changing safe houses daily. That suggested a man trading geography for time, trying to make a waiting game outlast our patience. He could hop provinces, hide in loyalist pockets, and let attrition do the rest. We did not have enough boots for a full occupation, and public tolerance for an open-ended presence was thin. For Saddam, the game was simple. Avoid capture long enough, and the world moves on. His two sons were also at large, and their reputations for unpredictability only made the stakes higher. We drove on, unsettled and empty-handed, the possibility of glory gone but the duty to keep looking still very much alive. It was—

A radio voice broke in: "Contact! Contact! Contact!" And we felt the first explosion a split second before we heard it. Nothing in front of us, so clearly it was behind us. It couldn't be a landmine; it had to be a ground attack. I grabbed the mic. "Report!"

The other seven surprised radiomen were all talking over each other on our radio net, and I couldn't make head or tail of it. Specialist Miller craned his head out our side window. "It's back there, sir. Definite incoming."

I raised my voice, appealing for calm. "Who got hit? What's the situation?"

More yelling, more confused sputtering. More explosions and gunfire.

"C'mon, people. Distance, direction, enemy? Give me something."

I may as well have been a hundred miles away. But I wasn't, and this whole thing was on me. I'd led us into an ambush. Now I had to get us out. I needed to be *back there*, on the ground, not a voice in their ears. I opened my door. Specialist Miller's eyes went wide.

The net dissolved into noise. The radios filled with half words and panic, like a kicked beehive. It was not that there was too much coming at me; it was that there was not enough. No bearing. No distance. No clear who, what, or how many. Information evaporated at the instant I needed it the most.

For a fraction of a second, a memory slammed into me so hard it felt like an impact: Ranger School, dark, cold, and a senior instructor looming over a trembling candidate. He loved that line, thin as a blade and just as sharp: "Whatcha gonna do, PL?" He would intone it, eyes flat, waiting for the platoon leader to make a choice that would either save lives or bury them. Saying it was a stress inoculation did not begin to cover it. It was a demand: Pick something and live with it.

The question landed and rolled past me like a stone in a river. I did not have the luxury of folding into deliberation. There was no map with neat arrows, no reconnaissance report folded into a pocket, no voice on the other end to hand me certainty. There was only me and the faces I was responsible for. I had led us into this valley of trees and silence; other people's breathing and futures were now balanced on the edge of my decision.

I threw down the handset. The plastic clacked against the dash like a final punctuation. The hatch popped, door flung open. Specialist Miller's head turned toward me, eyes that had learned radio brevity, but not this kind of movement. "Uh, sir—?" His voice tried to hitch to the plan, to the script. I did not wait for script or permission. I was already gone.

Running stripped everything else away. Adrenaline turned the world into a single narrow corridor ahead of me. The convoy blurred in a mix of tires, dust, taillights, and helmets. I vaulted over the last truck's bumper and hit the ground pounding, feet slapping the road, rhythm like a metronome set to urgency.

Distance shrank in my chest. I swallowed noise and tried to parse the smaller sounds: a clack of a magazine, a throat-roughened shout, the metallic staccato that meant gunfire, not fireworks. At vehicle three I barked orders, not because I had full context but because silence would be worse. "Return fire!" My words were anchors; they gave frightened hands a task. Task calmed panic, and action focused it.

Past Humvee five I saw shapes in the tree line—not a clear enemy formation, just flares of movement and the glint of reflected metal. The scene compressed and I felt simultaneously small and enormous: small because there was so little I actually knew, enormous because every second of delay multiplied consequences. Everyone was returning fire. Relief washed through me because somebody had found the firing positions, but the puzzle of intent remained. We had been hit from both sides. Violently—RPGs, machine guns. Where was the enemy assault that was supposed to follow? The trucks were vulnerable on the restricted terrain of the road. The lack of neat answers gnawed at me, but it also sharpened my next move.

I was not going to be a voice giving orders from the backseat. I was not going to be the man who watched his people pay for his hesitation. So I ran to the point where I could see, touch, and hear the fight up close. Presence. Not just command. If I had to be the one who swallowed the risk to buy others the space to breathe, then so be it. My boots kept time with my resolve.

Somewhere between running and taking stock, the old instructor's question solidified into a shape I could act on. *Whatcha gonna do, PL?* I decided. I moved. I aggressively moved toward the sound of fire to the best place for the leader in a firefight.

Finally, at Humvee six, soldiers were actually taking some initiative. It was my dismount squad, piling out just as I had, weapons at the ready, looking for targets. "I got muzzle flashes in the woods, moving, sir! Third Squad on me!" That was Tomkins, from Jersey, one of my best.

I didn't stop for a conference. "Roger, Sergeant!"

Then I was gone. At Humvee seven, ten meters beyond, a few soldiers were returning fire, but their .50 cal. up top was not. "Return Fire!" I bellowed to the gunner.

"At *what*, sir?"

"Any suspected enemy location, damn it! Like where you took fire!"

Burn marks and bullet holes streaked the metal of the convoy like angry tattoos. Spent casings from my soldiers' weapons crunched under my boots as I stepped, a metallic rain that kept time with my steps. When I got to Humvee eight, the incoming fire had ceased. Our last two vehicles had clearly taken the brunt of the attack from both sides, and a crazy amount of motor fluid was pooling out of Humvee eight and spreading across the road in a slick sheen of blackness.

Scattered full-auto bursts rattled the tree line, but I knew those were ours. My dismounts from Humvee six must have found something in the woods. Men were moving low and fast between tree trunks, weapons working, voices clipped and steady. There was no return fire.

I fought the urge to head over there and assessed Humvee eight first. "Tyrrell? You guys good?"

Sergeant Tyrrell emerged, shaken. "I think so, sir. Just...*whoa.*"

"We need to clear this vehicle. I think it is down, losing all fluids."

He got everybody out, no visible wounds, and when he opened the back, the mystery spill was solved: Incoming rounds had Swiss-cheesed a stack of fuel, transmission, and water cans. Anybody riding back there would have been dead. More shots from the woods. Tyrrell, his head back in the game now, nodded to our side of the road. "I can put a team up on that roof, sir?"

I squinted at what I took to be a deserted stable, then toward the woods. Someone from Humvee six was trotting back to us. When I waved, he paused. "Sir, I think you need to see this!"

What I needed to see was an abandoned enemy position—way too easily abandoned, from the look of it. Sitting blind up in the lead vehicle, it felt like the attack had lasted ten minutes, but it was probably thirty seconds at most. Lethal, to be sure: They had hit Humvee eight with RPGs, machine-gun fire, and light mortars, judging by the ammo left behind. But why would the terrorists dig in with heavy weapons, stage a textbook ambush on a convoy, only to ditch the operation within a minute instead of potentially wiping us out?

It wasn't just me who was mystified. The bigwigs at battalion were so concerned they told us to sit on the place. As in, prepare our *own* ambush on the assumption that our attackers would return. Strategically, it made sense. Humvee eight had slowed for a turn at a T intersection, a natural choke point on the hillside road to Hawija. The woods were close and thick enough to hide half a division. On the other hand, it wasn't like they dug bunkers and tunnels. Would guys too chicken to fight us that night come back to the very same spot?

We did as we were told. Every night, a platoon from our company was tasked to set up a welcome-back ambush. Forty Airborne infantry, lying in the darkness, waiting to unleash hell. Nothing happened. Night after night, the same routine. People began to think it was a waste of time, and resentment grew. And then one night I was sitting in our new riverside patrol base when the gates of hell opened.

"Enemy contact!" came the excited call over the radio.

They'd seen three men on foot, heavily armed, with RPG launchers strung across their backs. First Platoon let them walk right in, then gave them as much warning as they gave us that night—i.e., they opened up with everything they had and didn't stop until the fluids were pooling thick all around them. I got the call soon after. Scrambled my guys ASAP and headed over there with the commander to assist if needed.

By the time we arrived, the only help they needed was picking up the bodies.

Sometimes it's hard to look at people who've been shot to pieces, but this felt like justice because they were carrying tons of stuff, clearly intent on setting up the choke point for Round Two.

We were also surprised to learn they weren't Saddam loyalists. They were Kurds, the persecuted ethnic minority who hated the old regime even more than we did. Why would *they* attack us? Because Saddam's supporters had plenty of money and weapons but not enough men. And why risk your own skin when you can just hire somebody?

Which explained why our attackers had cut and run so fast that first night. They were paid to hit a convoy, but only well-trained professional soldiers willingly face injury or death. Bad guys in it for the money would rather live to see another payday.

In other words, we walked away unscathed that night thanks to basic human greed.

War teaches strange lessons. That night, survival came from greed, not heroism.

In the end, Saddam Hussein was not found in some fortified palace surrounded by fanatics or in a convoy racing across the desert. He was found near his hometown of Tikrit, in the small village of Ad-Dawr, living in a rundown farmhouse with no guards, no escape plan, no glory. Just a man hiding from the world. In December 2003, American soldiers pulled him out of a narrow hole in the ground, covered by a rug and dirt, with a pistol at his side that he never used. He surrendered without a fight. Operation Red Dawn, led by a joint special operations task force and the 4th Infantry Division, brought the Ace of Spades down.

It made me think back to that night near Hawija, just a ninety-minute drive from where Saddam was found to the farmhouse we raided on a whisper of intelligence. Had we been close? Could he have been there once, hiding in some hole we missed? Maybe.

But the truth is that it doesn't matter. What matters is that we acted. We made a decision. When others hesitated, we moved. You do not win wars, or lives, by waiting for perfect information. You win by moving forward, by making the call, by acting on what you have and what you know in that moment.

LESSON: TAKE ACTION

"A good plan violently executed now is better than a perfect plan executed next week."

General George S. Patton's words embody decisive leadership, the belief that movement, even imperfect, beats paralysis.

My mentors, like Leon and Liam, of course taught me about setting goals, but from a firefight to life itself, it always comes down to taking action. Good things come from movement. Nothing changes without it. Whether you are leading soldiers, teaching cadets, or facing a personal decision, waiting for the perfect plan is often just fear disguised as caution.

While teaching strategy at West Point, we briefly discussed a decision-making model developed by United States Air Force Colonel John Boyd known as the OODA loop: observe, orient, decide, act. Some people misapply Boyd's model to too many domains, from corporate strategy to grand military theory. But at its core it is a powerful reminder about the importance of acting. Boyd was describing a fighter pilot's rapid decision-making cycle, the ability to process information faster than your opponent and take the initiative. The one who acts first and adjusts faster wins.

I was taught to set goals and act on them, to be decisive. It matters on the battlefield, and it matters in life. Decisions, once made, create momentum. Movement creates opportunity. In war and in life, not acting is not an option.

EPILOGUE

GIVEN THE SCALE AND BRUTALITY of Russia's invasion of Ukraine, I was fairly certain it would be the defining armed conflict of the new century. Twenty months later, the far smaller irregular army of the terrorist political party Hamas launched a series of attacks of such shocking brutality that they too carved an emotional scar on the world for generations to come.

I'd done a fair amount of research in Israel prior to October 7, 2023, which now stands as the worst massacre of Jewish people since the Holocaust. On seeing those first reports of mass murders, mutilations, rapes, and kidnappings, I had a strong sense of what would happen next. Israeli defense forces would go into Gaza to destroy every possible aspect of Hamas, the greatest urban warfare challenge any military has ever faced against a massive and fanatical enemy force.

Hamas had been preparing for two decades, digging over four hundred miles of tunnels under their own population, whom they fully intended to use as human shields. The ruling power in Gaza, Hamas did not abide by any laws of war and had no concern for civilian life; that noncombatants would be killed was part of their strategy. Their forces could retreat, taking their hundreds of captives deep into their tunnel network, then bask as the world condemned Israel for their supposed "ruthlessness."

False assumptions quickly took root. That Hamas had committed "crimes," but Israel's response was "war," that Israel was invading a sovereign territory and unleashing a genocide.

None of which I found convincing, but I knew that once I got there, the true nature of Israel's military conduct would be writ large to any student of urban warfare. Accordingly, I lobbied my Rolodex of Israeli military contacts for access to study their Gaza operations as soon as possible.

Six weeks after Hamas struck, I'd arranged enough meetings to justify booking a flight...which meant I was trading in my Mr. Mom hat to go warrior-scholar again. It was getting harder as the kids got older. They saw the news. They knew where the hot spots were and what I did for a living. They had their own life dramas now and didn't need another parental absence to disrupt their routines. Between me and my ex-wife, they'd already had their share.

For our family bonding day before I left, I suggested a hike up the nearby Manitou Springs Incline, one of our family favorites. It is a local landmark in Colorado Springs, a hiking trail that follows the route of an old funicular railway that washed out years ago, about 2,768 steps that climb nearly 2,000 feet in elevation. I have seen plenty of strong-looking adults turn back halfway, which is why I have always been proud that my kids have made it to the top with me for years.

For us, the hike is more than exercise. It is a kind of ritual. The military taught me how the body and mind connect through shared challenge, and while I do not put my kids through Ranger School, those climbs have become our own form of training. A little hardship, a little sweat, and a lot of conversation. Some of the best talks I have ever had with them have been on that trail—about goals, fear, perseverance, and the difference between giving up and just taking one more step.

Each time we climb, it feels like the distilled essence of everything I have tried to pass on: strength of mind and body, kindness, respect, ownership, perseverance, and the truth that nothing worth having comes easy. The incline is our shorthand for life itself. We start at the bottom together, we climb, we get tired, and we keep going because the only way to the top is forward.

Which is not to say they just scamper up there like mountain goats. As in Ranger School, there has been the occasional whine, foot drag, and "Daddy, I have to go to the bathroom!" But just as Sergeant Hall once coached me to stay in the game when I was sure I was done, I take a knee and counsel my darlings on the creed of Don't Quit. Life will throw so many challenges at you and the best way to prepare is by doing hard things and seeing them through, whether it is the Manitou Incline, the classroom, or the sports field.

We distilled it all into a Spencer Family Code some years back, which I am proud to say has provided us all with purpose and commitment when times get tough. We developed it when their mom and I were still married and she was deployed to Kuwait, Iraq, and Afghanistan. I was struggling to parent three young kids, ages seven, five, and three, who missed their mom deeply. I needed something to tell them when they were struggling. The code captures the wisdom I have acquired in my lifetime, a blueprint I never had growing up.

We made it to the top that day, the four of us winded and our calves aching, but breathing in that clear mountain air, looking out over a beautiful country that seemed endless. I took a long look and held my babies extra tight because I knew my next stop was hell on Earth.

Standing there, I felt the familiar tension between two callings: the father who wanted to freeze that moment of peace and the soldier-scholar who knew he could not. The world was at war again, and I had a duty to witness it, to study it, and to tell the truth about it. The lessons I tried to teach my kids—strength, courage, perseverance, and service—were the same lessons that pulled me back into the field.

A few weeks later, I was on a plane to Israel, preparing to enter Gaza.

As I described in chapter 1, you can easily travel to Israel, but getting into Gaza is tough. Arriving in early December 2023, I started making the calls I hoped would provide me access, as well as picking the brains of officers throughout the Israeli Defense Forces. What I learned that most surprised me were their efforts to *minimize* Palestinian civilian casualties—in that I realized Israel was not just adhering to the accepted war standards set by international law but was going above and beyond to safeguard civilian lives and property. These unprecedented efforts include providing warnings to civilians prior to attacks by methods never used before: phone calls, texts, voicemails, and drones with speakers. They put out flyers that included the IDF's own military maps and directions to safety corridors. They offered daily pauses in fighting from the opening weeks of the war. There was also a determined effort to use arms and munitions that would minimize collateral damage and casualties. If that strikes some people as performative or window dressing, I assure you it is not.

Critics claim the IDF has wantonly destroyed and killed on an epic scale. This is simply not true. Had they intended mass destruction, that power is entirely at their disposal. Gaza has not been flattened, and her people are not marked for annihilation. Those who think that Israel "overreacted" to the October 7 attack need to understand how war has traditionally been waged within our lifetime: the defeat of the Axis powers in World War II and how the standards or laws of war have evolved since then. What my research in Israel has proven to me, over multiple visits during the war, is their concern for human life and a sincere commitment to minimizing civilian misery.

"But, John," cynics may gasp, "I saw a pool of blood in a bombed-out *school* on TV!"

No one can deny that endless horror show, all seemingly real-time evidence of atrocity. What the media *doesn't* provide enough of, in my opinion, is the context of such attacks—nor is there proper vetting of the reported damage or what Hamas was doing in the building that was once a school or mosque. That blood people saw may or may not have been a child's; that rubble may *not* be a school. Casualty figures tossed around by outraged talking heads often seem pulled out of thin air. "No, no," the media replies haughtily, "we got that from a *solid source*." But dig into that solid source a bit, and suddenly things don't feel all that solid.

My research in Gaza is no different from the other conflicts I have studied. But given America's deep cultural ties to Israel, far more people seeking analysis of the war saw my reports in their newsfeeds through *Time*, *Foreign Affairs*, *The Wall Street Journal*, *Newsweek*, and many others. Any discussion of Israel draws an inordinate number of eyes, and most of the feedback I have received has been positive. Still, there has also been a sharp rise in blowback. While my research may challenge people's beliefs, there is nothing political in what I do, which makes it all the more dismaying that I have been drawn into the endless left-versus-right arena.

I had discussed my findings on television many times before, but in August 2024 I faced one of those moments that truly tests your composure. During a live CNN interview, the host tried to cast me as an Israeli surrogate, citing reports from writers with little experience in urban warfare and no understanding of the ground. I kept my cool. Years of research and walking battlefields had taught me to stay calm under fire, whether from bullets or bad questions.

That being said, my new "fame" hasn't all been crushing. On a follow-up trip to Israel in February 2024, I received the rather astounding message that the prime minister wanted to meet with me. My first thought was I was in trouble—*Did I reveal something I shouldn't have?*—though that's hardly something a world leader would handle. More likely it was just a headline/photo op—*Netanyahu Greets War Researchers*. There'd probably be a line of us. We'd go in one by one, shake hands, a few words, smile for the camera, and out.

Arriving at the appointed time at the prime minister's office, my processing through security made it clear this was no pool event. Nor did I have time to worry in the waiting area, where I was met by one of the prime minister's primary advisors. Ushered through an open door soon after, we were greeted by Prime Minister Netanyahu himself, who got up from his desk and came around to shake my hand as we stood for a photo with a world map in the background. Assuming I would then be ushered out, I was again surprised when the leader of Israel said to me, "Have a seat," indicating a set of leather chairs around a small coffee table.

I sat. You can see my "deer in the headlights" look in the picture we took.

"So," the prime minister said pleasantly, "tell me about yourself."

I blinked. *Really? He brought me in for a friendly chat?*

Well, two can play that game. Without belaboring things, I briefly explained I was a poor kid from the sticks who became an Army Ranger, then worked my way up to teaching at West Point, and that I now do war research. Mr. Netanyahu nodded in recognition. I knew his career likewise began in the IDF special forces.

His foreign policy advisor was holding the copy of my book *Understanding Urban Warfare,* which I'd brought as a gift. Again, to my surprise, the prime minister asked to see it. Scanning the table of contents, he asked about some of the famous battles I described, which led us into Gaza. From his informed tone, I realized he'd actually read my recent articles. If my initial responses were briefing-room terse, once it became clear I'd been invited for a frank exchange, not an interrogation, I relaxed, and the facts flowed more easily from my brain to my tongue. The prime minister was particularly interested in historical analogies to Gaza, and I explained the parallels with the brutal US battle to retake Manila from entrenched Japanese forces in 1945, as well as lessons drawn from US experiences in Seoul, Korea, in the urban battles of Fallujah and Ramadi, and from advising and supporting the 2016–2017 fight for Mosul. I assume we spoke longer than scheduled, as after some staff throat clearing, their boss finally rose, warmly thanked me for coming in, and told me to "keep up your important work." As a parting gift, he gave me a copy of his memoir, pausing to write this dedication:

> Col John Spencer,
>
> In deepest appreciation for your stalwart defense
> of the truth,
>
> Benjamin Netanyahu

Those words mean a lot to me.

Fighting for the truth is one of my core values, and bringing the truth to light in *this* conflict was all the more important, given Israel's maligned status in the court of public opinion. Even so, I left in a bit of a daze. I've spoken about my work to people from all walks of life, but a head of state is truly echelons above reality.

In fact, my tour had just begun. My next appointment was with Lieutenant General Herzi Halevi, the head of the IDF, whom I had written about but never met. Our discussion focused on the broader scope of military objectives, and once again I was treated with genuine respect. The meeting concluded with the general's remarkable acknowledgment that I was on my way to meet one of his division commanders, Brigadier General Dan Goldfus, who was operating in one of the toughest areas of Gaza, Khan Yunis. He smiled and said, "I hope your research goes well."

Like the prime minister, General Goldfus began his career in special forces. While Netanyahu had served five years of active duty in Israel's equivalent of the US Green Berets, General Goldfus had spent his career in Israel's version of the Navy SEALs. In person, he was a force of nature, the six-foot-two embodiment of IDF intelligence and determination. Speaking English with a South African accent, he was at first more gruff than his politically attuned superior, but as our conversation moved deeper into the realities of urban warfare, he began to speak more openly about the hard lessons of recent operations. I had been formal and reserved in the offices of national leaders, but in General Goldfus I found a fellow warrior-scholar, a commander who constantly studied both the science and the art of war. He spoke of Carl von Clausewitz and the enduring principles of maneuver warfare. Our quick rapport was evident, and one of his aides later remarked with surprise, "I can't believe how much he told you."

All this high-level access was both humbling and motivating. My sense was that while these leaders had all the intelligence they needed, good commanders still sought outside perspectives and understood the professional value of independent research. I was likely chosen because of my extensive record of academic work and demonstrated integrity, a student of their challenges who was unencumbered by any government title or political agenda.

I later interviewed the prime minister for my research more than once during the war. War is the pursuit of political goals, and as a researcher of war, the chance to ask a head of state about the objectives given to the military and the critical decisions being made is an opportunity few people in the world have ever had. The real highlight came five months later when he cited my work by name during his address to the US Congress—saying, "John Spencer, perhaps the world's greatest expert on urban warfare, says…"—and again nearly a year later during his speech to the United Nations.

I couldn't believe it. By any measure, it was the capstone of my career. Sure, my kids were unimpressed, but my sisters were very proud. Not long after, I was also mentioned in debates in India's Parliament and in senior leadership discussions in Azerbaijan. Each time, it felt surreal.

Of course, this great career event brought an unforeseen consequence—a target on my back. Some people now think I'm Israel's hired stooge. The innuendo has surfaced in many quarters, including *The New York Times*, which sent its own version of Lois Lane to dig into my past, questioning my expertise, my research, and my motivations. In the end, there was no hit piece on me. Maybe they discovered that I truly am an expert, motivated by values rather than whatever they were hunting, or maybe it will run later. Like every challenge I have faced, I take it day by day.

Now I know what you may be thinking as we come to the close here. "Hey, good for you, John. All your pain and misery paid off. You're sitting in the big chair, with the grown-ups, and that's your off-ramp from the highway to the danger zone. No more 'almost dying' for you."

Well, now, hold up a minute.

There's actually more to the General Goldfus story.

As we discussed the IDF's efforts to locate Hamas tunnels, he mentioned "camera drops." When I asked about that term, he turned to his aide. "Do you have his vest and a helmet ready?"

A minute later, we exited the building and hopped in a jeep that drove us across the sand outpost to the general's command vehicle. Which wasn't a black SUV or an IDF Humvee but a Namer—essentially a tank with less firepower and extra armor. He showed me in, gave me a seat, and the driver wheeled us out the main gates. Within minutes, we'd crossed the border into Gaza. Fifteen minutes after that, we entered an urban area. I had no clue where we were. Finally asked.

"Khan Yunis."

It was the place we'd just spent an hour discussing, where his troops had fought hardest; a notorious terrorist stronghold, honeycombed with deathtraps. As you may have noticed, I visit places like Kyiv, Shusha, Kfar Aza, Sderot, or Mumbai—where violent clashes recently took place, *not* during the actual battle itself. Now, suddenly, I was in a war wagon, infantry crammed in around me, powering into a zone where heavily armed killers would definitely regard us as a primary target. I flashed back to 2003, leading my Humvee column through the ruins of Iraq. Instinctively, I reached for my hip, that security of just touching my weapon; only I wasn't a combatant anymore, just an observer. People ask if I go into these situations armed. I do not, mostly because if things really got hairy, I could just pick up something.

Wherever the Namer was headed, we were taking a lot of hard turns. On the gunner's video monitor, I watched us skirt piles of rubble and squeeze through narrow passages between high buildings. We passed other IDF vehicles, dismounted squads, blocks and blocks of rubble. Then I heard gunfire. Heavy machine guns and RPG booms. Sounds I remembered in my bones, sounds you never forget, the sounds you pray you'd never hear again.

We came to a sudden halt. Down went the ramp, and we emerged into stinging daylight. It was a four-way intersection with tanks blocking the other three avenues, bombed-out buildings all around, and that gunfire *maybe* a block away, a scene straight out of a WWII movie.

General Goldfus strode forth, shoulders back, knowing exactly where he was going. Down the northern street, past the sentry tank, regular troops regarding him in awe, the Big Boss taking a spin around the factory floor, and me stifling the urge to hug the wall as I followed him. Bounding, in fact. The general's security detail would trot half a block ahead, grab cover, scan, then motion us forward. Moves I'd performed a million times, but never as a civilian. I felt both out of place and in a familiar dance.

Two turns down side streets brought us to a sort of public square facing a heavily damaged mosque. Scoping the panorama, I saw IDF troops on the watch with a small group huddled at a far corner. That's who we'd come to see. As we crossed toward them, I pegged them as combat engineers. They had a drill mounted on a small two-wheeled trailer, about the size of an outdoor lighting rig, grinding straight down into the ground. Once they'd gone down about fifty feet, a camera attached to a fiber-optic cable was slowly lowered down the inch-wide hole, and the engineers saw what the camera did on a monitor. This was the technique the general wanted me to see. IDF teams were sinking a hundred cameras a day; once discovered, the Hamas tunnels were quickly breached, investigated, and destroyed.

The men performing this high-tech recon were older. Reserve forces of the IDF usually are older, but there was a group standing by that looked a lot younger as well. When they noticed me looking, one of them approached, introduced himself in perfect English, and explained they were officer cadets of the Duvdevan, the IDF's special operations troops. I was surprised. This was frontline combat duty, and there's nothing more dangerous than rooting out a deeply entrenched enemy, but Israel believes exposure to real-life scenarios is invaluable for training tomorrow's military leadership. In a way, that aligned with our mission at the Modern War Institute, to let the next generation walk the actual ground, to study the latest developments in warfare *today*, not simply absorb the lessons of the past. Only these IDF students weren't just walking the ground; they were actually *in* combat and on mission. The policy of allowing them to learn while doing would pay off spectacularly in Gaza when a class of armor cadets killed the Hamas leader, Yayah Sinwar, during a firefight in Rafah. And, as I later found out, we *were* standing directly on top of a Hamas tunnel that day. Had their spotters decided to ambush the camera droppers or blow any booby traps that Hamas often rigged up inside the tunnels they'd abandoned, we could've easily wound up as collateral damage.

We spent the rest of the day visiting other units under the general's command during their operations. In one instance feeling the building shake as an armor brigade commander explained the challenges he was facing from Hamas guerilla-fighting techniques. The general and I withdrew unharmed that day, but sadly, two IDF soldiers died in an IED blast there a few hours later, on one of the very streets we'd traveled. I don't know if they were among the men I rode in with, but they could have been.

That's about as close to the action as I want to get these days.

So is this really the end of the road for me almost dying? I'd assumed I would face less danger when I retired from active Army service, but fate has a way of coming back to bite me—so who knows what hot water the future has in store for me.

There's also the small matter of the death threats.

Oh, I didn't tell you? That's part of the fun of being in the public eye. Apparently, a number of shadowy but profane operatives intend to inflict unspeakable mayhem upon me, so stay tuned. *The* Next *Twenty Times I Almost Died* could be even more action-packed!

LESSON OF ALL LESSONS

I have a question I like to ask people and groups. When I was in the military it was, "Who are we?" It was a question about our values, about the Army Values, our standards—not only the ones required by rules and regulations but also the standards we held ourselves to. Our norms.

Now I ask not only myself but others: "Who are you?"

At first, I usually get puzzled looks. Then I tell them there is no wrong answer. I also tell them I will go first. I am a father, a brother, a son, a Ranger, a writer, and a scholar. I am a man who lives by a set of principles, values, and morals about right and wrong.

I think the drill is important.

I have learned a lot in my twenty-five years of active-duty service, in my years as a war researcher, and from the twenty times I almost died. I was blessed with countless chances to show who I was, to stand up for the truth, to help others, to lead soldiers in combat, and to raise children (a work in progress). I learned that I am not defined by one identity. I am not a one-legged stool. Everyone needs identity and purpose. Neither is singular. Both are necessary.

I also learned that neither identity nor purpose matter without values. Values are the foundation of who you are, what you do, and who you choose to stand beside.